DESIGNING AND
BUILDING MODEL RAILWAY
BASEBOARDS

DESIGNING AND BUILDING MODEL RAILWAY
BASEBOARDS

Ron Pybus

THE CROWOOD PRESS

First published in 2015 by
The Crowood Press Ltd
Ramsbury, Marlborough
Wiltshire SN8 2HR

www.crowood.com

British Library Cataloguing-in-Publication Data
A catalogue record for this book is available from the British Library.

ISBN 978 1 84797 869 1

Disclaimer
The author and the publisher do not accept any responsibility in any
manner whatsoever for any error or omission, or any loss, damage,
injury, adverse outcome, or liability of any kind incurred as a result of
the use of any of the information contained in this book, or reliance
upon it. If in doubt about any aspect of railway modelling, including
electrics and electronics, readers are advised to seek professional
advice.

Designed and typeset by Guy Croton Publishing Services,
Tonbridge, Kent
Printed and bound in Malaysia by Times Offset (M) Sdn Bhd

CONTENTS

ACKNOWLEDGEMENTS

Thanks are due to the following for allowing me to take photographs on their premises or of their layouts, and to include them in the book as detailed below:

B&Q Chippenham – timber cutting
Elite Baseboards – construction of their baseboard
K. (Harry) Harper – railway room layout (Penbooney)
John Langley – TV-based layout and briefcase layout
Model Railways Solutions – construction of their baseboard and helix

Jean Morgan – car roof top box layout
North Cornwall & Devon Model Railway Club – table-top baseboard
John Roxburgh – garage-based layout
David Shephard – loft layout
Dave Simpson – railway set (The Gas Cupboard, Trowbridge)
Mark Tucker – garden shed based layout
West Wiltshire Model Railway Circle – wall-mounted board and set of basic boards.

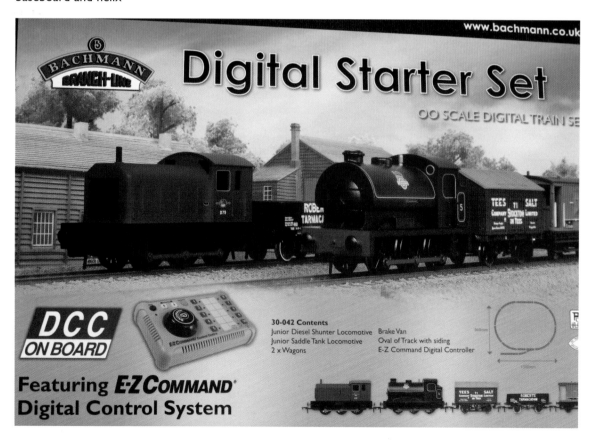

Typical initial train track set.

INTRODUCTION

It is probably fair to say that the majority of people who have any involvement with model trains, in any shape or form, started off in their childhood with a small train set given as a present at Christmas or at a birthday (*see opposite*). The usual scenario when the child's interest was brand new, would see the box being opened and the various contents removed. Having looked at all the rolling stock, the next stage would be a rush to clip the track together to form an oval. This was usually initially done on the floor or on a table covered with a protective cloth.

Track was easily clipped together and two tags were used to connect a battery powered simple controller. At the end of the session, the track would often be unclipped and put back in its box until the next time it was brought out and the process repeated. It was usually not very long before a point was added, thus creating a siding with the addition of a few more lengths of track. At the end this meant even more dismantling and I remember from my childhood that after a few outings, interest declined a little as the construction and dismantling, plus the occasional separation of the track during operation, reduced the time spent playing trains. This increased as the odd tunnel, signal and station were added, thus complicating matters even further. It is usually after only a couple of weeks before some sort of more permanent layout is required, so that the track can be put away, both safely and quickly, after each running session, and, in addition, there were usually fewer derailments when track was permanently fixed to a board.

The vast majority of people were introduced to model railways with the 'OO'-gauge scale. In the 1950s 'OO' was seen as a downscaling from the larger sized clockwork trains of earlier times. In the twenty-first century the 'N' gauge has developed dramatically, both in quality and reliability, and this, coupled with smaller houses being the norm, has led to an upsurge in this smaller gauge. However, 'OO' gauge is still the most popular. From the Far East have come the even smaller gauges of 'T' and 'Z'.

The same rules of baseboard design and construction apply to all. The bigger the gauge, the greater the size of the layout and the greater number of baseboards required to accommodate the same track layout. With 'O' gauge there is a need to provide greater stability and greater strength to the baseboards than with other gauges, purely because of the weight of the locos and rolling stock. In practice this can be achieved by slightly increasing the thickness of the baseboard top and ensuring adequate lateral strapping.

Without some form of baseboard, 'playing trains' will never expand to railway modelling and interest in the train set will decline over time.

CHAPTER ONE

GETTING STARTED

Railway modelling has many and varied interpretations and objectives. Some people just have an interest in running trains around a simple layout; others are more interested in getting as much track as possible on to any baseboard. Other people are more interested in creating an overall scene through which model trains happen to run, whilst still others are interested in reproducing a specific location and year in absolute accurate detail. Some are mainly interested in shunting wagons, whilst others prefer a main-line operation. Some want end-to-end operation, but others require continuous operation. Whilst American rolling stock and massive layouts are ideal for lots of modellers, there are just as many, if not more, who are only interested in British stock or even just Great Western locations and stock. The choice is yours. There are a range of modellers who are pushing the boundaries and creating layouts in a variety of containers and there are those who compete to create a layout that is more compact than any other.

Just as there are a wide variety of types of interest, there are almost just as many track sizes, from TT and Z gauges, through N and OO, HO and O, as well as all the narrow-gauge and fine-scale variations that exist. To the newcomer there is a bewildering array of choices and always someone on hand to tell you that their choice is the best, the most realistic, the most widely available, and so on.

One aspect that brings everyone together is the need for a solid baseboard on which to build a layout. This book is a guide to the design and construction of a variety of types of baseboards for railway modellers. It cannot be totally comprehensive as every single modeller with have his or her own needs for their layout in their situation.

As you have selected this book it is fair to assume that either you have decided to move on from a simple track that is taken up after each use and to put it on a more solid structure, or, more likely, that you wish to move into railway modelling with all that implies.

This book will take you from the very beginning through to the design and construction of a completed baseboard or set of baseboards for use in the home or for exhibition purposes.

Railway modelling requires a wide range of skills at different levels. These include design, choice of materials, woodwork, wiring, electrics, soldering, scenery construction and painting. This book will deal with all the skills required in the construction of the most important part of a model railway – the baseboard.

A baseboard is like the foundation of a house: if you do not get it right there could be movement, either vertically or horizontally, and the operation of the trains will continue to create problems. It has always been the case that the baseboard should support the track and be totally rigid. In the past this was achieved by using heavy timbers, especially if the layout was to be a permanent fixture. Modern thinking has totally moved to lighter and thinner materials, using effective design to provide the rigidity in just the same way that motor cars have moved away from a solid steel chassis to a lighter monocoque construction for their rigidity.

It is unlikely that any one person will have all the skills required for all aspects of model railway construction and operation, but knowledge and skill can be gained in a variety of ways. It is hoped that this book will see you over the hurdles of baseboard construction. Help is available from other sources. There are numerous monthly magazines and also a range of simple pamphlets on almost every topic you can think of. You can buy commercially constructed baseboards in a variety of stages of completion. Your local model railway shop is also an excellent source of help, but the widest range of assistance can be obtained by being an active member of your local model railway club. Most clubs will have a membership with a wide spread of expertise and members who are willing to help each other. If you share your expertise with others, they will share their expertise with you.

Another great source of information is the series of model railway shows. By visiting a show, you will be able to see a variety of different baseboards in use and you will be able to chat to a multitude of enthusiasts who will be able to give you a wide range of tips and guidance. It is also an opportunity to make contact with local club members, so that when you go along to your first club meeting you will already have made contact with several members. Local shows are far more use than the big national shows, as you will have greater opportunity to meet local people and they will have a greater opportunity to spend a little time with you. Some clubs have their exhibition layouts totally designed for exhibition viewing and their members are keen to explain to anyone asking; but there are others who admit to using exhibitions as an infrequent opportunity to run a full layout and have little interest in making it entertaining for the paying public. If you feel you are not wanted, pass on to the next layout where you will more than likely receive an enthusiastic welcome. I gained most of my initial knowledge from visiting shows and then quite a bit more from joining a local club. Even now I still gain information from shows and local club members.

Only recently I helped a member construct half a dozen baseboards, which had been purchased in flat-pack form and we both learned a great deal. This book, although designed to help you in the construc-tion of your own baseboard, does have a section dealing with the problems and pitfalls of commer-cially purchased baseboards.

Finally, you can often purchase a second-hand baseboard via eBay or some other source. Just like buying a second-hand car, there are pitfalls and things to check out before committing to purchase, and these are also covered in the book.

I have constructed several baseboards specifically to allow me to illustrate this book and I have shown, in the detailed construction instructions, that there is more than one way of achieving the end result. In the descriptions of the basic, flat-topped baseboard, and the instruction on construction of the folding base-board, I have shown two entirely different ways of gluing the cross-members in place. There are other examples of different methods of construction and you will probably find that you will discover an alter-native to what is suggested in the book. My aim is that the book will have given you the information you need to construct a variety of different base-boards. I have kept strictly to baseboard construction and only referred to track design and layout as a source of information to enable the boards to be constructed.

The boards described are all designed for continu-ous running in N gauge, but for end-to-end running or for OO gauge the sizes of the board will vary, but the basic construction methods and requirements will be identical.

I hope that this book will guide you through all the pitfalls and enable you to make decisions about what you want to build and how you want to construct it. If, having used this book as a guide, you build a layout that is easy to operate and meets all your require-ments, this book will have achieved its objective.

CHAPTER TWO

THINGS TO CONSIDER WHEN PLANNING THE DESIGN OF A LAYOUT

PREPARATION IS THE KEY TO SUCCESS

I cannot stress too strongly that preparation is the key to success in designing a baseboard. A multitude of things have to be considered. There will be a variety of constraints and layout requirements, as well as storage, portability and cost implications to be considered before starting a layout.

There are people who have a small layout and just want a board to keep it in place, both when operating and when it is being stored, and there are other who will react more to the space available and how they can fill it to the absolute maximum. The vast majority have an idea in mind and are prepared to work within the constraints that are unique to them to achieve the outcome they require.

The whole of the planning stage can be just as interesting, exciting and brain-taxing as the actual construction. A poorly planned layout will soon result in a lack of interest in operating the finished article or cause problems in actually achieving on the board exactly what the owner has in mind. By trying to fit too much on to a board it is possible to make the curves so tight that some of the longer locos will slip, as friction between the wheel flange and the rail is greater than the forward thrust of the drive friction on the track.

In planning a house an architect has to plan its size, how the various services will be fed into the correct room and how the materials available are best used to achieve the desired effect. In some cases building a house will require ground excavation of a wider area than the footings for the property. The railway modeller is not only designing the layout of the track, but the whole rural countryside or urban scene, and these facts have to be considered before the board is designed. Just as with a house or street of houses with its mass of underground drains, water, electric and gas supply pipes, a model railway will have wiring to cope with electrifying the track, point motors, polarity, signals, lighting and so on. Wires will have to pass through the baseboard at certain points, and point motors will have to have the actuating rod in exactly the right position to couple with the point-switching bar. The last thing you need is for a point-motor's position to coincide with a cross-member or a joint underneath the baseboard, so detailed layout plans are essential prior to starting to build your baseboard.

When deciding on the size of the baseboard there can be a tremendous cost-saving by ensuring that wood is available in the size required, or making slight modifications to the size of board you require. If you decide you want your baseboard to be 620mm (24½in) wide, there will be considerable wastage as sheets only come in set sizes, and so you might have to buy a 1,220mm (48in) wide board, whereas reducing your layout to 600mm (23¾in) would exactly fit the width of a standard sheet of ply or MDF and have little effect on either the overall design of the layout or the tightness of any curves. Fortunately, most sheet timbers relate closely to imperial measurements, so, for example, matching up to existing imperial boards is not too difficult. The wrong thing to do is to build your boards without planning exactly what you want and how it will best fit on the planned board, only to discover a whole host of problems through lack of forward planning.

WHERE WILL IT BE STORED?

As with the size of sheet materials, you need to plan out where it will be stored when not in use. If it is to be a permanent fixture, there is no problem with storage as it will remain in one place, but in many cases rooms have to have dual purposes these days. The spare bedroom is the usual location of a layout, but what happens when guests or relatives come to stay? If it is stored correctly it will suffer less damage than if it is just pushed into a corner.

If it is to be fitted into a wardrobe, for example, it needs to have a baseboard of a size that will both go through the door and be slightly narrower than either the width or depth of the wardrobe in question. It also may have to be carried up stairs and round bends, so it needs to be sufficiently compact and lightweight to be easily handled. Later in the book you will find construction details for what I have described as a 'folding baseboard', which has been designed to fit both in a storage cupboard and in a car.

It may be that you are planning to hinge your layout to a wall so that it can be folded up when not in use; this will mean strengthening the side where the hinges are fitted, as one side will be supporting the whole weight of the layout on two specific points and at 90 degrees to the normal stress point.

WHERE WILL IT BE DISPLAYED AND OPERATED?

No matter where it is displayed, the baseboard should not detract from the overall quality image of the layout; in fact it should be something that exists, but is not really noticed. An intrusive baseboard is a wrongly planned or wrongly designed baseboard.

In its simplest form, layouts aimed at children are often operated from a dining-room table. Obviously, the size of the table is a constraint on the size of the layout. The baseboard will not need legs, but there will need to be some protection between the bottom of the layout and the table top. The sides of the baseboard need to be sufficiently deep to accommodate wiring but, more importantly, point motors. If a cloth or rug is placed between baseboard and table, there needs to be an ample gap between the bottom of projections, such as the actuating bar of the point motor, and the table protector. Depth of the frame should be at least 60mm (2½in). All wiring will have to have connections through the side or on the top surface of the baseboard to ensure that the

Free-standing layout in a 'den'.

Layout in a train room – 'Penbooney'.
K. (HARRY) HARPER

Typical garage layout. JOHN ROXBURGH

board lies flat on the table, even when transformers and controllers are attached.

If the baseboard and train layout are to be operated in a bedroom, you will need to provide some cover to protect the layout, track and scenery from a gathering of dust. It will also either be fixed to a wall, or more likely, free-standing. If it is fixed to the wall and goes all the way round the room, some form of access will be required by the door, or it will have to be an end-to-end layout rather than a layout with continuous running, unless each end is increased to permit the creation of a 180-degree curve. I would strongly advise against fixing any layout to the wall unless you plan to fold it up against the wall. It is far better to have all the units free-standing, not only so that the room can be redecorated with ease, but so that each board can be stood on end for initial wiring or for subsequent maintenance, without having to scrabble underneath.

By far the best option is a dedicated 'train room'. Even in such a room I would still strongly recommend that the baseboards are free-standing, for the reasons quoted above. Some people will have the luxury of a 'spare room' that the 'powers that be' will allow to be used for railway modelling. Use of a spare room keeps all the railway material confined, it provides a static location, giving greater reliability and, above all, it will be heated, thus giving greater encouragement to spend time with the layout. A garage dedicated to the railway is also a good location, as long as heating is provided and as long as a car is not sharing the space. A wet car, parked in a garage overnight, is far from ideal!

Garden-shed railway room. MARK TUCKER

Layout in garden shed. MARK TUCKER

The dedicated space could be round the walls of a garage or in the loft. There are many cars that are parked on the drive with the garage being dedicated to the model railway. This is especially true of the 'O'-gauge layouts where a large area is required, and if you can take over a double garage, so much the better.

In the past, the simple garden shed has been the home of many a layout, but with the introduction of solid wood interlocking chalets and home/office insulated wooden sheds, the scope has increased dramatically. In either garages or any form of shed, some form of heating and a de-humidifier is almost an essential, if damage is not going to affect the layout.

FREE-STANDING OR WALL-MOUNTED?

I have previously said that if at all possible the baseboard and layout should be free-standing to allow ease of access and for maintenance. There is more than one layout I know that is hung from the ceiling and is lowered using a cranked pulley system. Hanging from a flat wall at the appropriate height, with drop-down legs on the outer corners, is another alternative, which, for smaller layouts (up to six feet long), has the advantages of a free-standing

layout, in that it can be lifted for repair and maintenance underneath, whilst at the same time being easy to stow away. With the right frame and cover it can become an almost invisible part of the room and its décor. Care has to be taken that the layout stands sufficiently far out from the wall to accommodate the height of the scenery when the baseboard is in its vertical (closed) position. The alternative is to have all the buildings removable.

Wall-mounted layout in the open position.
WEST WILTSHIRE MODEL RAILWAY CIRCLE

Wall-mounted layout in the closed position. Note the temporary upright locking system of a wooden batten screwed to a convenient beam. This system will be improved in the near future. WEST WILTSHIRE MODEL RAILWAY CIRCLE

LAYOUTS IN THE LOFT

In older houses there is usually a large, open loft area that can be used to install a model railway. In more modern houses the construction of the roof trusses prevents the use of this area. If you have a loft, there are several factors to consider. In a normal loft there is a considerable depth of insulation (usually over 250mm/10in) at floor level. Lofts will have a tremendous variation in temperature from sub-zero in the winter to the high thirties °C in parts of the summer. To make an effective railway room from a loft will take a considerable amount of work. In many lofts the original joists are not sufficiently strong to provide the support needed and cross-beams will have to be laid at 90 degrees to the existing trusses and then floor boarding will have to be laid. If you do not ensure adequate strength, you will no doubt find cracks appearing in the ceiling below as the structure flexes. The ceiling will require 50mm (2in) or 100mm (4in) insulation board to be fitted between the rafters and you will probably have to fit insulation board to create the walls of the new railway room. All this is time-consuming and quite costly. You also have the problem that all your materials have to pass through a small ceiling hatch to which has been fitted a loft ladder. Whilst it may be a big space, it is fraught with costly difficulties. Subsequent difficulty of access often means that use of the layout is limited, and the older and more infirm you become, the use is reduced even further.

A layout in a loft. DAVID SHEPHARD

TRANSPORTABLE LAYOUTS

I have already suggested that all baseboards should be sufficiently light to be removable, to allow for redecoration of a room, the arrival of visitors or the storage of a layout between it being operated. This section deals with those layouts designed to be transported on a frequent basis; for example, a club layout that has to be regularly transported to a village hall in time for club meetings; but most of all for transporting and erecting at exhibitions in a wide range of different venues. Exhibition layouts tend to be constructed on multiple boards.

The key factor is that they should be light enough to be carried by one, or at the most, two people. Second, they should be of a size that will easily fit in a car, as well as being secure and unable to move around in an emergency. Multiple baseboards can either be stacked on top of each other or they can be carried vertically alongside each other. (*See* section on Designing for car transportation in Chapter 3.) It should also be remembered when planning the

Transport boxes. Each box holds one baseboard and the units fit across the rear of the vehicle. The larger of the two boxes carries the baseboard with its background attached; the upper box carries the baseboard with its background removed.

The detached background bolts to the top of the upper unit when transported.

A pair of legs slotted into sockets underneath a baseboard. They are stiffened with a cross-member at both the top and the bottom of the leg.

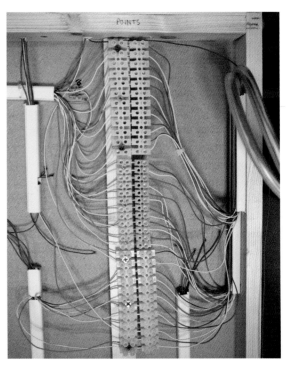

Plugs and sockets are used to transfer wires for track, points, lighting, signals and so on, from one board to the next or direct to the power source.

design of the baseboard that it may be necessary to carry a second operator in the car. The depth of the baseboard should be sufficient to protect any working parts underneath the layout, such as point motors, signal motors and other sub-baseboard items, from any damage. In other words, the sides of the frame must be deeper than the point motors and their actuating arms or the base of a mechanically operated signal. To gain space it may be sensible to have a removable background (if the landscape contours and buildings on the layout are sufficiently low level to produce a space gain) otherwise, retaining the background will provide protection to the layout.

Ideally legs should be totally separate to the baseboard. First, they add weight and, second, if they fold they usually manage to open and snag on the car or on other layouts when loading and unloading. Such layouts should either be designed to be placed on tables or the legs should be able to be attached on site, either into each baseboard or to create a 'table' on to which the baseboard is slotted.

There must also be a safe way of storing electrical connections during transport and during assembly. Usually this is achieved by the use of one of a whole range of plugs and sockets.

Protection from the rain needs to be a consideration, as transport from a car to a school hall or similar during heavy rain could dramatically affect the electrical integrity of the circuits or affect the scenery. Often protection is achieved with a simple sheet of plastic, but care must be taken not to damage any vertical structures.

WHAT SPACE IS AVAILABLE?

Layouts vary in size from shelf size to full-room size. Smaller layouts that fit shelves or fit an alcove in a living-room or bedroom must fit in with the décor of that room and the subsequent layout must be able to be accommodated within a fixed space. Full-room layouts can be as large as the room, but take care: it is far better to start small, with perhaps two boards, and gradually grow the layout, rather than trying to lay it all out at once. You need to design the whole layout, but creating any layout of any size is a considerable expense and takes up a considerable time. Similarly, baseboards can be made one by one, as required, as long as the connection between the two boards is carefully planned.

HOW HEAVY WILL THE FINISHED LAYOUT BECOME?

With every layout, weight is an important factor. A properly constructed baseboard will be fairly lightweight and will support everything a model railway constructor will put on it. If the layout is to be almost permanent, weight is not significant; however, even in such cases, it is sensible to have heavier structures that are removable. There are a multitude of plaster-cast buildings, which are excellent but they are weighty objects and ideally should be set into the scenery in a way that they can be easily removed and replaced if any movement is to take place.

Often modellers strive to make the baseboard as light as possible, sometimes with the loss of strength or rigidity, by leaving out cross-members, but then they proceed to add unnecessary weight with a variety of heavyweight pieces of scenery.

DESIGNING THE TRACK BEFORE YOU START BUILDING

I cannot stress too strongly that it is important that you have a track design planned before you actually start building your baseboard. There is nothing worse than finding that your concept will not fit effectively on the board you have built. Obviously, this book on the design and construction of baseboards does not deal with the design of layouts. It is vital that you have a detailed plan of exactly where the track and everything is going before designing the construction of the baseboard. Commercial baseboards have fixed positions for cross-members and the spine, and in these situations, the track plan has to work round the design of the baseboard. In making your own baseboard you have control of where the cross-members and spine are positioned. Track cannot be positioned very close to either the sides or the end of a baseboard if a point motor is to be fitted below the baseboard. Likewise cross-members should be located to be clear of any point motors. The exact spacing of cross-members is not that crucial, nor is the spine position. If you are building on more than one board, it is best to keep the number of tracks that run between boards down to a minimum. The more you have, the more you have to ensure that they all line up perfectly. (*See* Chapter 4 on layout design.)

A full-size track plan drawn out on lining paper before being transferred to the baseboard. The track plan should be produced at a very early stage to permit the accurate placing of cross-members and the central spine.

CHAPTER THREE

SIZE CONSTRAINTS

METRIC VS IMPERIAL MEASUREMENTS

It has to be said that the vast majority of railway modellers were brought up in the age of feet and inches being the only measurements and a good percentage have continued to work in imperial measurements to this day. I am regularly asked for the size of my layout when it is being requested for an exhibition and I always give the metric measurements, only to be asked, 'Can you give the size in proper measurements?'.

In building a baseboard it will be essential that you work in metric. There is little point in seeking wood marked 2in x 1in or, worse still, asking your supplier to cut wood to imperial sizes. The young people manning cutting equipment were brought up being taught metric measurements and they are much more likely to make a mistake if they have to convert. It does not help you to stay imperial at the end of the day because timber is all pre-cut or pre-planed to metric sizes. By working to imperial sizes you can easily find yourself purchasing larger pieces of wood, especially in sheet form, than you would if you were planning in metric. It also complicates matters when selecting wood. If you know you need a 3ft length of 2in by 1in for the side and you need four such lengths, you then have to work out whether this can be obtained from 2.4m lengths of timber, usually whilst you are in the shop.

It is far better to work it all out in metric in the first place. *All measurements in the book are primarily metric, with approximate imperial equivalents.*

ACCESS ALL AREAS

In constructing a layout it is important to ensure that, when completed, it is possible to reach the back of the layout from the front. It can become necessary to reach over to the furthest track to make some correction and you just cannot do this if the baseboard is too wide. It is generally felt that 700mm (28in) is the maximum width to allow you to reach everywhere on the board.

TRACK AND POINT RADII

The overall width of the baseboard is governed, in the majority of cases, by the tightness of the curve you wish to employ. In the main this constraint applies to continuous-running circuits, where there have to be 180-degree curves at each end. The radius depends on the length of the loco, the location of the track (track in a yard or shunting area can have tighter curves than on a main-line) and the scale of the track. The more modern locos, and some of the specialist carriages, cannot cope with anything less than almost maximum radius. The absolute minimum 'N'-gauge radius is 230mm (9in), with the main-line radius being 380mm (18¾in). In 'OO' gauge, the minimum is 475mm (18in) and the main-lines radius is 915mm (36in).

Given these measurements, it is possible to begin to work out the size of the baseboard width, always allowing for the track to start at least 15mm (½in) in from each side, in order that point motors, etc., do not foul the side frame of the baseboard.

Even if you are planning to build an 'end-to-end' layout, the space between track and the point size will have an effect not only on the width, but on the length. The majority of modellers find that length is more of a problem than width. Especially when planning a siding, it is vital to ensure that you have sufficient space from the point to the end of the track to accommodate all the rolling stock plus the loco, without the train fouling the points. If you have multiple points leading into several sidings, space seem to disappear at an alarming rate.

The gradient of the slope required to raise a track to a different level, especially where it crosses over another track, must be considered. It is generally considered that a gradient of 1 in 50 is about right on a straight track with about 1 in 60 on a curve, so it is best to put risers on a straight stretch of track.

DESIGNING FOR CAR TRANSPORTATION

Exhibition models and club models regularly need to be transported and this is usually achieved in members' cars. If you know that you are going to have to transport your layout at some stage, it is important to design it so that it can be easily accommodated in a variety of cars. Unfortunately, all cars have different loading spaces. It is much easier now than it was in the past when most cars had a traditional boot. Today the majority of saloon cars have a pair of fold-down rear seats, and some have totally removable rear seats or at least seats that fold flat into the floor. The average width of most boot areas is just over a metre, but length will vary according to the type of car, hatchback or estate. I would always recommend that layouts are built on baseboards that fit across the width of the car. If you do this and change your car, you either have to ensure that your new purchase has sufficient width, or ensure that at least what went across in the old car will fit lengthways in the new car. It is far better to design a layout that has a snug fit, rather than one that rattles around. This is more important if you have more than one baseboard and need to stack one on top of the other.

Stacking can be achieved through the construction of a frame that rigidly supports one or more baseboards, or by a series of boxes into which each baseboard and its layout fits.

Two boxes (made to fit the width of the car as well as the height width and depth of each baseboard) provide easy storage and good protection when the layout is being transported. They can be carried into a venue to protect the layout from rain, if necessary. The layout with the fitted background is shown being slid into the transport box. The background has been fixed, as the height was needed for the coalmine winding gear, which is just visible.

MULTIPLE BOARD LAYOUTS

If you cannot fit your planned layout on one board, you either have to add additional boards or re-plan your layout. It is simple enough to add additional boards but it brings up a whole host of technical challenges (see Chapter 10).

The greatest problem with having more than one board is ensuring that they join together in exactly the same position time after time. The smaller the gauge of model, the more accurate it needs to be. Fastening two boards together can be achieved in a variety of ways, the most common of which is a couple of bolts with butterfly nuts. Unless the hole is protected, the wood will gradually wear and the joint will become slack, allowing upward and side-

ways movement. This can be overcome by the use of a suitable diameter hollow steel rod inserted into the appropriate end of both baseboards. Another method is with toggle clips to hold the baseboards together. These have the advantage that you do not have to scrabble under the baseboard to find the locating holes. The third choice is to use hinges where the central pin can be removed to permit separation. All these are adequate methods of joining boards together but to ensure exact registration each time, you need to fit male and female dowels to the joining edges. The cheapest are made of wood, the next best are brass dowels, which require a drilled hole in each baseboard, but by far the best, and unfortunately the most expensive, are brass pattern-makers' dowels.

Cutting the steel rod to provide protection from continued wear and to ensure reasonably accurate alignment.

Tapping home the rod into the pre-glued frame.

Place glue in the hole that has been drilled to allow the cut rod to be fitted securely.

The steel rod in place ready for the bolt.

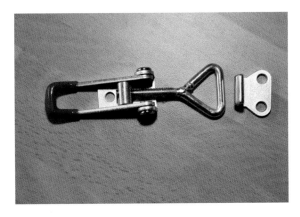

The toggle clamp ready for fitting to the side of the frame to compress the two frames together. Adjustable clamps allow the contact pressure between the boards to be adjusted.

Track wiring will have to be connected between the boards to ensure continuity of supply. Also, power supply to points, lighting and other electrical accessories, e.g. signals, must be linked across the boards in some way.

STORAGE OR DISPLAY SPACE FOR MULTIPLE BOARDS

Brief mention has already been made of the need to plan storage before embarking on construction, but if you are having multiple boards, you need adequate space to either store the boards when not in use, as well as protecting them from damage, or, if they are part of a permanent or semi-permanent display, you need to ensure you have sufficient space both for the boards to be displayed and for access to them both for work and for viewing and keeping them apart during storage.

TRANSPORTABILITY AND SCENERY

Often it is not the problem of transporting in a car or van, but manhandling the baseboards from one site to another and then positioning them to permit accurate joining. Baseboards these days, as will be demonstrated, can be made to be rigid but fairly light. The mistake often comes when scenery is added. Cast models of houses, shops and so on, must be removable, as each unit is quite heavy. Using plaster bandage to make scenery is also much heavier than papier-mâché or polystyrene as the landscape base. The height of the scenery is also a controlling factor. Tall mountains, etc., should be removable and any protruding item should not be too close to either the back or the front or either side of the individual baseboards. I made the mistake of having a station platform near the front with people sitting on benches and I constantly have to stick them back as they become knocked as I stretch across the layout when transporting it.

Platform and people. The mistake of putting the platform too close to the front of the board regularly resulted in people or signs being knocked off when the layout was being transported. I now use a bulldog clip to fix a strip of wood to the front when transporting.

CHAPTER FOUR

DESIGN YOUR LAYOUT FIRST

PLAN FIRST – BUILD SECOND

There is a simple rule when cutting wood, 'Measure twice – cut once', and this is equally true of any work on a baseboard. The planning needs to be meticulous to allow for a simple, trouble-free construction. Skimp the planning and you will pay the penalty throughout the construction, and possibly throughout the life of the layout.

There is no point in having a rough sketch. You need detailed drawings showing exactly where the track fits, how steep the curves are, where there are rises and falls, where the platforms fit and whether the coaches and locos will cope with the proximity of tunnels, bridges, buildings and platforms, before you begin any construction. You need to ensure that there is enough room for a head shunt or whether the platform or goods' yard will hold appropriate numbers of rolling stock.

It is not just the track, but also the electrics: you need to ensure that you can easily wire in points, lights, signals, etc., in a neat and obvious way.

One longer term consideration is whether the proposed layout will give you sufficient satisfaction when it is being operated. If it only has one siding plus a single circuit, you will find it lacks interest after a while. On the other hand, putting too many junctions and sidings or too many running tracks can complicate a layout until it becomes too complicated to work. There are many computer packages that help with design but, at the end of the day, there is nothing more accurate than a full-sized template.

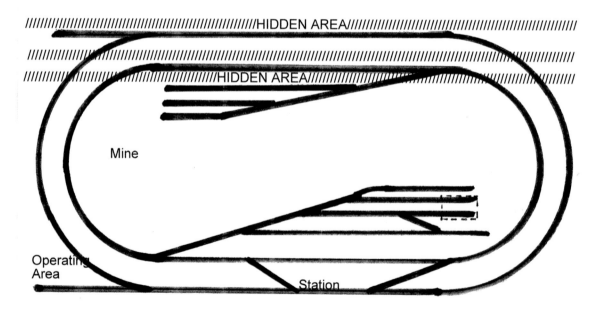

Layout plan marking hidden areas, station and so on.

PRODUCING A FULL-SIZED TEMPLATE

The simplest way is to purchase a roll of lining paper from a decorator or from one of the DIY stores or even a 'pound shop'. An alternative is to find a commercial catering outlet and buy a roll of paper table-cloth, which is usually 1,000mm wide. Most people opt for the lining paper as it is far more readily available. The first thing to do is to cut your roll to the exact size of the planned baseboard. This will probably mean joining two pieces side by side for a continuous layout, as lining paper is only 530mm (21in) wide. You can obviously join the two with Sellotape, but that is difficult to draw on, or you can use masking tape or just glue each edge together. Either of the latter two options allows continuous lines to be drawn.

The initial step is to draw lines to represent the outer frame, which will obviously run around the perimeter of the baseboard. The lines should be drawn in ink, so that they are clearly visible when planning your layout.

Next you need to draw thin pencil lines to show the ideal position of the cross-members and central spine, which will be underneath the board. They should be drawn to exactly halve the board width-wise and then the cross-members should be positioned approximately 300mm (12in) apart and an equal distance from each other and the sides.

As I have said these are ideal positions but the whole point of drawing up the full-scale plan is to permit modifications before any cutting is undertaken.

Before you start work on the full-sized version of your layout it is best to use an A4 pad to produce a variety of sketches to help you decide which layout best meets your requirements. Once you have an almost finite design in mind, start to transfer it to the full-sized plan. You must work lightly in pencil as your design will have to be adjusted as you begin to fit things into place. If you have difficulty in designing

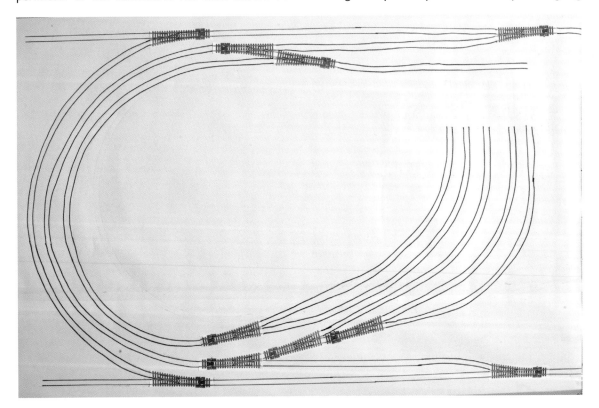

A different layout plan, using turnout (point) templates and Tracksetta gauges plus a ruler.

A variety of track plan guide books.

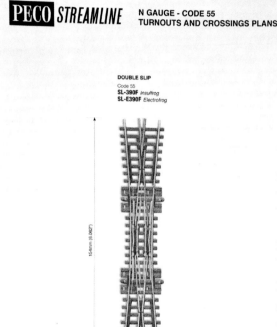

PECO crossover plan.

a track plan, there are a multitude of books on the subject or, better still, you can gain valuable visible operation of a variety of layouts at one of the many shows around the country.

Once you have pencilled out a track line you need to ensure that you have no potential problems with point motors being directly in line or very close to the projected position of the central spine or cross-members, or, if it is a multiple board layout, that points do not come close to a join. By making some adjustments you will be able to move cross-members or points in one direction or another so as not to be on a join. If it is possible, move the point to a position where there are fewer rail joints between boards, as each joint is a potential problem area, no matter how much care is taken.

If points come in line with a cross-member or the central spine, it is best to adjust the position of these cross-members or the spine so that they do not coincide. All it means at this stage is rubbing out a pencil line and moving it until it is clear of the obstruction above, then redrawing the line representing the cross-member or central spine.

Once you have this completed this, you need to make sure that you have all the angles and curves correct. It is usually best to start with points and PECO are helpful in that, if you go on to their website

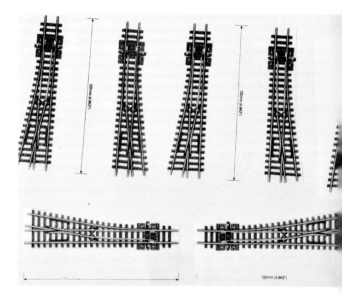

PECO turnout plans.

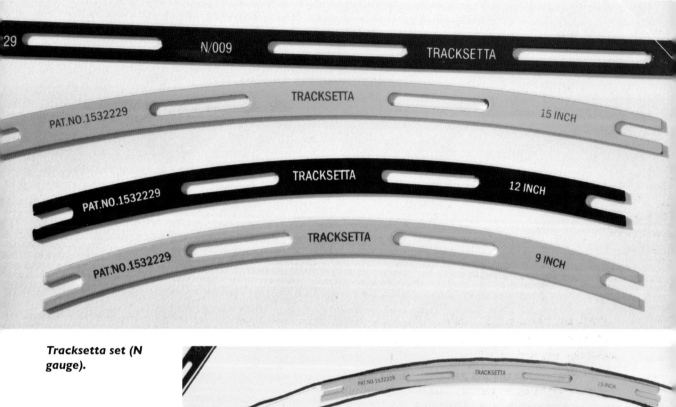

Tracksetta set (N gauge).

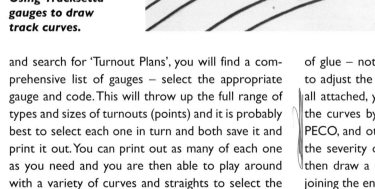

Using Tracksetta gauges to draw track curves.

and search for 'Turnout Plans', you will find a comprehensive list of gauges – select the appropriate gauge and code. This will throw up the full range of types and sizes of turnouts (points) and it is probably best to select each one in turn and both save it and print it out. You can print out as many of each one as you need and you are then able to play around with a variety of curves and straights to select the most appropriate for each junction. Place them on the draft layout.

Once you have what you feel is a satisfactory layout, it is best to attach each printout with a dab of glue – not too much, as you will probably have to adjust the position at least once. When they are all attached, your next move should be to draw in the curves by using the 'Tracksetta' templates that PECO, and others, produce. You need to decide on the severity of the curve and its exact positioning, then draw a soft pencil line along each side, finally joining the end with either a point or another curve until you have the full track.

If you are having double, parallel tracks, you need to use a '6ft way gauge' to ensure separation. On tight curves you need to allow a greater space

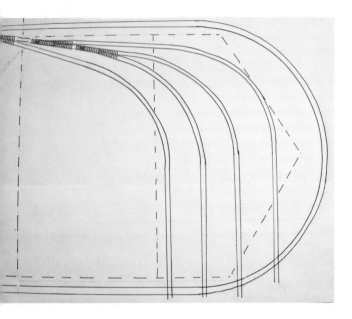

Completed track plan showing cross-member positions (dotted lines).

between tracks than a way gauge indicates. To test, line up the two longest coaches on opposite pencil tracks and attach a pencil to the front outer corner and lightly score a line with the pencil. Do the same with the other coach, but with the pencil in the outer middle. There needs to be a gap between the two lines, otherwise the coaches will not pass. The same work needs to be done with platform edges and with buildings and bridges, which is why it is not just the track that has to be planned in detail but also all the buildings.

Only when you are sure that you are happy with the layout should you go over pencil lines with ink.

From this full-scale drawing you will be able to work out your track requirements and, more importantly, the exact sizes of your wood in order to produce a cutting list. Once you have compiled these lists, you can put the plan in a safe place until you have the baseboard completed.

Using a coach to check clearance on a curve – drawing a line following the front corner of a coach when on a curve.

Using a coach to check the clearance on a curve – drawing a line following the centre of a coach when on a curve.

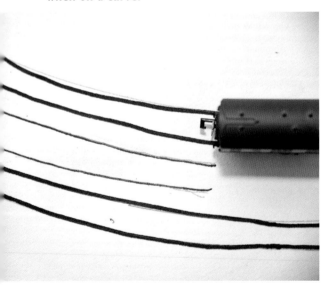

Resulting lines showing clearance of passing coaches.

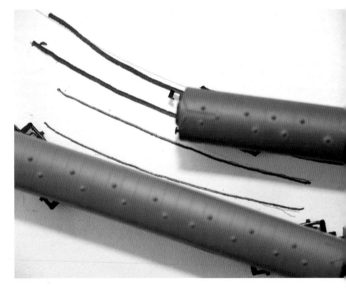

Coaches laid on proposed lines showing clearance on a curve.

Later in the book you will find that you need to sketch the layout of the cross-sections on to the baseboard, especially if the cross-members and spine are not 100 per cent symmetrical. Having exactly calculated your track and point requirements, it is probably best to order them as a complete lot and negotiate a discount for the bulk purchase, rather than buying track and points bit by bit.

CHAPTER FIVE

TYPES OF BASEBOARD

Over the last decade or so there has been an increasing interest in baseboard experimentation. Looking back over thirty years, baseboards were heavy and made of thick wood or chipboard, but the world has moved on as a result of modern technology and experimentation. Some of the attempts have been purely pushing the boundaries to see what can be achieved, others have been based on the need to reduce weight following the increase in movement of baseboards between exhibitions, or between houses as people move or just, with smaller houses being the norm, to make them easier to put away and store.

This chapter will run through a variety of baseboards to give modellers an idea of what is out there and at least to stop them reinventing the wheel or creating difficulties for themselves.

THE SOLID WOODEN BOARD

In the past, the usual first board for a simple oval or similar model layout was a piece of 4ft (1,220mm) by 2ft (610mm) of fairly heavy board. The track was usually laid on top and points were either manually operated or operated by electrical point-motors mounted on top of the baseboard. This style of board, even for the simplest of layouts, has gone out of fashion, in part because it was so heavy and in part because thicker sheets of wood are now expensive. Chipboard and blockboard are often used for such boards but they are extremely heavy. Chipboard is probably the worst material as it is rough, slightly uneven and will easily break at the edges if not protected.

The simple solid wood baseboard. The photograph is of the North Cornwall and Devon Club 'OO' test track laid out in the village hall, rented for monthly meetings.

THE EGG-SHELL (OR HONEYCOMB) DOOR

Early lightweight doors used to be made out of two pieces of hardboard with a paper honeycomb in the gap, with the four edges being made of thin strips of wood. In more recent times, the hardboard has been replaced by thin (about 3mm) plywood. Whilst hardboard had a tendency to warp and had some flexibility, plywood has slightly improved stability. Such boards are fairly light, but have fixed sizes (1,980mm by 700mm or 840mm/78in by 27½in or 33in), which can make layout design, transport or storage a little difficult. The boards have the problem that point motors have to be fixed to the top surface, but wiring, with care, can be fed through to the underneath. Feeding wire to the underneath creates the problem that the board must be raised slightly when operated or wires will be scuffed or pulled out. Egg-shell doors are now not as popular, as fashions have changed and panel or grained doors have taken their place as a cheap door.

INSULATION BOARD

Sheets of Celotex or similar insulating materials have, on occasions, been used successfully as lightweight surfaces on which to lay a track. The use of such materials has been more popular in the United States of America than in Britain and Europe. The material is extremely light and it is easy to cut holes to take point motors and to feed wiring. It is also less noisy than any of the above. However, unless it is protected, it is very easily damaged. Joining boards together also creates problems. In some cases protecting the lightweight material is achieved by adding 6mm (¼in) or 9mm (³⁄₈in) thick plywood wooden sides. If they are slightly deeper than the foam-board, the sides protect the wiring to some degree, but effective joining can only really be achieved if the foam-board has both ends and sides covered in plywood or softwood. In effect, the foam-board eliminates the need for cross-members and a central spine, and in my opinion creates more problems than it overcomes. Track also needs to be glued down, as pins tend not to hold too well.

The 'honeycomb' of a door with the outer skin removed.

Celotex 50mm insulation board ready to be inserted in its frame.

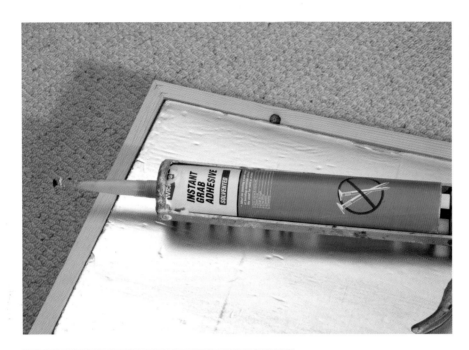

The Celotex glued into the frame with a typical grab adhesive, which does not 'melt' the foam insulation.

WOOD AND SUNDELA

This has been the traditional way of constructing baseboards. The standard has been a 50 x 25mm (2in x 1in) frame with a spine and cross-members roughly 300mm (12in) apart. Sundela has the advantage of easily accepting pins to fasten the track, but it has the disadvantages of its weight, the need to protect the edges from damage and its tendency to warp slightly over a period of time, especially if moved between locations with different humidity levels. Our club have just removed several discarded layouts from the loft of our rented premises. Several sheets of unsupported Sundela were stored with about 600mm (23½in) overhanging, and after storage in the loft, although perfectly dry, the sheets have drooped and created a 90-degree bent sheet.

In more static layouts, modellers have laid Sundela on top of plywood. The reasons for doing this appear to be to reduce running noise (plywood will 'drum' as a train runs on the tracks) and to permit pins to be easily inserted when fixing the track. The disadvantage is the increase in weight.

WOOD OR WOOD AND PLYWOOD

There are really three main types of baseboard in common use. The most popular was a wooden frame and wooden cross-members and a wooden spine. The advantages of a wooden frame is that it is easy to cut and join together, and it comes off-the-shelf in pre-set sizes, only requiring cutting to make it the right length. It is important to ensure that the wood is straight when you purchase it, as wood can have a slight warp depending on how it has been stored, transported or displayed. When you get it home, ensure you lay it flat and preferably lay something heavy on top of it, as the change in temperature and humidity between a store and home can be quite dramatic and encourage the wood to warp. Most wooden frames are constructed in PSE (Planed Square Edge) wood that is 18mm (¾in) wide by either 44mm (1¾in) or 69mm (2¾in) or 75mm (3in) deep.

More popular today is a wooden frame but with plywood cross-members and a plywood spine. The wooden frame, as already stated, is easier to construct, but using plywood for the spine and cross-members reduces not only the weight of the board,

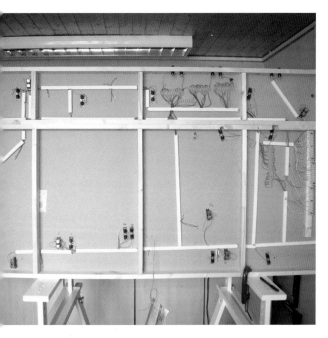

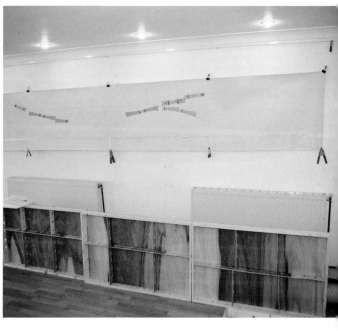

Typical wood frame and wood cross-members on a baseboard in the process of being wired.

Three wood-framed boards with plywood cross-members and spines. Note the layout plan on the wall to ensure that cross-members do not interfere with point motor positions.

but also, as the plywood is thinner, it reduces the problem of point motors and other fittings under the baseboard competing for the same space and compromises having to be made.

PLYWOOD

Commercial baseboard suppliers mainly use plywood. They have the advantage of having jigs set up to cut

A typical all-plywood commercial construction.

B&Q in-store woodcutting machine.

corners accurately and to drill pilot holes, which makes the whole process more accurate, but home construction from scratch is within the scope of most reasonably able DIY modellers, with a limited amount of simple equipment. It is made even easier by many of the large DIY retailers offering a cutting service. Using such services provides you with the accuracy of professional cutting at little or no extra cost. It also means that you can select large sheets for cutting, as the ready cut results will fit in a car, whereas a full sheet 2,440mm (96in) × 1,220mm (48in) requires larger transport facilities. Using the full-sized sheet can halve the cost of purchase of the required materials. Side frames are usually 9mm (^{3}/$_8$in) thick, whilst spines and cross-members can either be 9mm (^{3}/$_8$in) or 6mm (^{1}/$_4$in), with a top of 6mm (^{1}/$_4$in) for most boards.

MDF (MEDIUM DENSITY FIBREBOARD)

It is not recommended that MDF is used for the frame or the cross-members, as it has a limited ability to take screws into any end. It is used by some as the surface of the baseboard, but has a very slight tendency not to remain perfectly flat and, more importantly, cutting it creates a massive amount of very unpleasant dust. It is also much heavier than the same thickness of plywood. The cost-saving on a large sheet is less than four pounds. Pinning track tends to be more difficult than with plywood, as the fibreboard tends to expand slightly into any drilled hole.

NOVELTY BASEBOARDS

A baseboard can be made out of any material that will support tracks and in a quest for something a little bit different to exhibit, several modellers have resorted to layouts installed in briefcases; another has resorted to using a large car roof box. A Wild West layout in an old computer monitor cabinet is yet another variation, but the quirkiest I have seen was a toilet and cistern, with the track running round the rim of the pan and through the cistern. I am sure that there are many other novelty layouts, which I have not seen.

Novelty layout in a metal briefcase.

Layout in a car roof box. This particular layout has a gimmick of a noisy, fast-running pig running round one of the tracks.

A Wild West layout in a former computer monitor.

COOPERATIVE BASEBOARD CONSTRUCTION

Just expanding into this country is FREMO. The group has existed in Germany for over thirty years and is a large group of international railway modellers who come together from time to time to operate a series of modules, which have been constructed by individual members in different parts of Europe. The key is the use of totally standard end pieces, so that any end piece can join with any other end piece on a totally different member's module. Each end piece has standard jointing holes and standard track locators. On one occasion, members joined together to make their layout 1.2km (¾ mile) long. Apart from using standard end plates, the remainder of the construction is up to the individual.

Additionally, there are the beginnings of a movement by one or two board manufacturers to produce a standard end panel. Dapol have also become interested in such a project, as well as one or two 'N'-gauge

groups. My own club has recently started to construct two totally new layouts and, in particular, the 'N'-gauge section is planning to develop a new club layout, into which can be inserted two additional boards for use at exhibitions. The front-of-house part of the layout will consist of individual members' baseboard sections, which can be brought together to form a continuous-run layout, both in the clubroom and at exhibitions. This requires totally standard end plates, so that any board can correctly link with any other board. We are planning to have a local metalworker produce a metal jig to guide drills, so that ends can be produced, but we are also hoping that we can find a manufacturer who can produce end plates for us, as well as marketing them nationally. It seems as though there is an interest and lots of complicated specifications are circulating, but no-one has bitten the bullet and produced a product. The first one with a viable, reasonably priced product will probably capture the market. Only time will tell and hopefully this section will be out of date soon after this book is published.

Sample end board masters produced by 'FREMO'.

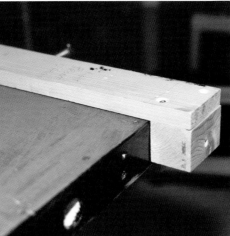

ABOVE, FROM LEFT TO RIGHT: *My wooden jig, so that my boards have a standard fit. The jig fits over the end of each baseboard (left or right) and has two holes to allow the insertion of a pilot bit to ensure dowel holes are centred and match each board. The jig showing one of the pilot holes.*

OPEN BASEBOARDS

Having constructed the basic monocoque frame and cross-members, it is possible to add plywood tops only where the track and buildings are to be located, leaving the remaining area open. The open areas are covered by scenery, which does not require too strong a support. The higher levels of scenery can begin to be sculptured by the addition of taller cross-members or the addition of taller formers joined to the existing cross-members. Using this method is probably the best if you are having multiple levels of operational track. The main baseboard construction chapter (Chapter 7) demonstrates such a construction, as well as construction using a totally flat top.

The open top board has its cross-members cut to match the shape and contours of the area and has small flat areas on to which the track beds, made of 6mm (¼in) ply, are screwed and glued. The frame is softwood. The open areas are filled with scenery without any solid base.

CHAPTER SIX

TOOLS

It is possible to construct baseboards using only a few manual tools, but the use of one or two powered items will make the task so much easier. Using DIY stores or building suppliers who provide a cutting service will reduce the amount of sawing that is required and provide you with far more accurate cuts than can be obtained at home, unless you have a well-equipped, semi-professional workshop. The better quality the tool and the more appropriate it is for the job, the better will be the result. If, for example, you are inserting pin nails, you should use a small hammer, not a large one, and a rotary sander will not get into corners as well as a detail sander, but if you only have a rotary sander it can be used in combination with a little hand-sanding.

CUTTING SOFTWOOD

As I stated earlier, PSE (Plain Square Edge) softwood comes in standard sizes. Making a softwood frame will only require you to cut the wood into the appropriate lengths. To achieve this you will require a tenon saw with 12 teeth per inch, a mitre block and a set square.

Tenon saw with a minimum of 12 teeth per inch.

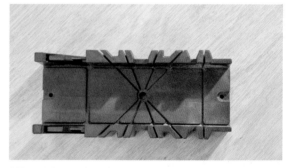

Mitre block showing the variety of cut angles available from 45-degree mitres to 90-degree square cuts. It is important to use such tools each time rather than guessing.

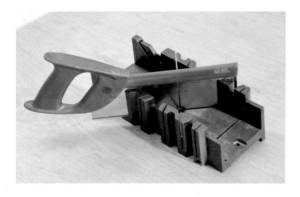

Mitre block with tenon saw.

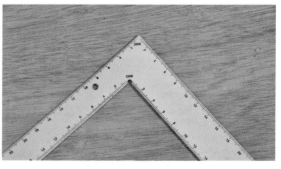

Set square with both metric and imperial measurements.

Electric chop or mitre saw. Using such tools is much quicker and slightly more accurate.

The use of a powered chop saw or mitre saw will provide a more accurate result, more quickly and with less effort, but hand tools are perfectly adequate to achieve an excellent finish.

CUTTING PLYWOOD

Cutting plywood into strips that are over a metre in length and only 50mm (2in) or 75mm (3in) wide is not easy using a hand saw. If you are sawing by hand, the blade of the saw needs to have at least 10 teeth per inch to achieve a fine cut. The cutting line needs to be well defined and the whole of the plywood sheet needs to be fixed firmly, with the small strip also being supported when cut. Circular saws with a fine blade will produce far more accurate cuts than a jig saw, but jig saws can be used with care and with a firm guide clamped parallel to the required cut.

Jig saws are best used for curved or intricate cutting, not for straight lines. There are a variety of wood cutting blades. For straight lines use the widest blade, but keep to small-toothed blades rather than rip blades.

Electric saws are useful for cutting long lengths of wood, but they must have a fine-toothed blade or the underside of the wood will tend to splinter.

Jig saws are useful for cutting intricate shapes or short lengths. For intricate cuts, use a narrow blade.

Jig saws can be used for long lengths of plywood, if necessary. Use a wide blade, as this will tend to hold a straight line more easily, and clamp a length of wood so that the sole plate can be pushed against the clamped wood to produce a perfectly straight cut.

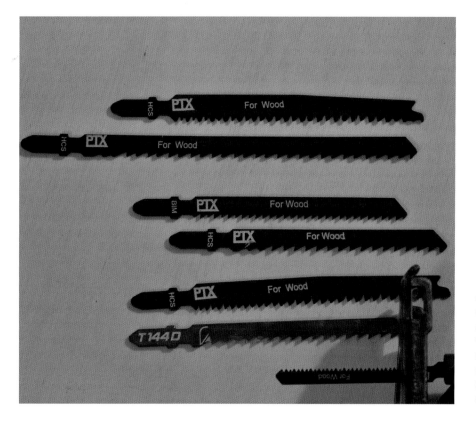

A variety of wood-cutting blades. Note the different widths. The blade at the bottom (in the jig saw) is best used for cutting curves.

Cutting service at a builders' merchant. It is essential to have a cutting list, a cutting order and preferably all the measurements in metric because, although all the machines carry both measurements, many of the operators are young enough to have only been taught metric measurements. It is best to carry your own tape-measure with dual measurements so that you are able to check the accuracy of the cuts.

The most accurate way is to have the sheets of plywood cut when you purchase it. Large DIY suppliers, and some builders' merchants, offer a cutting service and this will be detailed in the next chapter. It is important that you carefully work out not only the sizes of plywood required, but also the cutting sequence, as the commercial machines cut in a variety of different ways. It is important to talk to your supplier before finally drawing up a cutting sheet. You need more than just a cutting list, you need to work out the exact cuts required and the sequence of those cuts, otherwise you will be purchasing more wood than you actually need. They will cut in the most simple way for themselves and this may not be the most economic for you. I admit that I rarely cut plywood myself, but rely on the DIY shop's cutting service.

SANDING WOOD

Once all the wood has been cut to size it will need sanding down to take off all the rough saw edges and also to smooth out the flat surfaces. This can be achieved with a sanding block and hand-sanding or, better still, with a power sander. These can be a belt sander, a sheet sander or a detail sander. Which you use will vary as to what you own or the price you are willing to pay. A belt sander will sand large, flat areas but will be difficult to use on edges and corners, whereas a detail sander will easily cope with edges and corners, but will just take a little longer with large, flat areas. Fortunately, baseboards are not really too large and I usually use just a detail sander.

Orbital or plate sander. These are ideal for sanding large areas but because they vibrate in a circular pattern, you cannot get completely into corners.

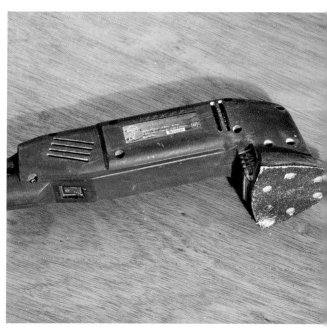

Detail sander. The sanding plate has a similar shape to the plate on a domestic iron, and can reach right into corners and, as baseboards are not that big, can easily cope with the flat areas of a baseboard top or underside.

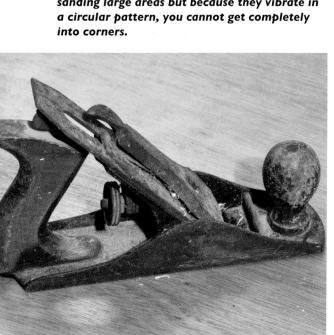

A hand plane can be used to shave off any excess on baseboard edges (although, if you have measured properly, they should not exist). With plywood, they do have a tendency to splinter the edges unless the blade is extremely sharp.

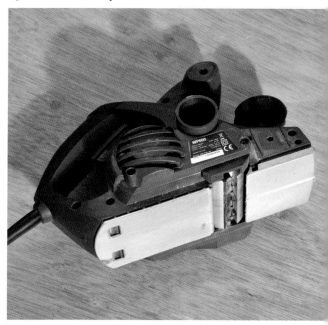

The electric plane does the same job as the hand plane but is much kinder to plywood. You are able to skim off minute layers of wood with only minimal edge damage.

The Surform is basically a hand rasp and is yet another way of removing excess wood. Used gently and pushed from the edge down towards the baseboard, there should be little damage to the edge of plywood.

Sandpaper should be the only item needed if you have made your frame and baseboard top accurately. Rough sandpaper is ideal for the start of any sanding process, but for sanding prior or during the painting process, fine sandpaper or even finer glass paper is all that is needed.

If there is a difference between the frame and the top, for example, which requires more than sanding, you can use a hand plane, a rotary plane or a Surform tool. If you have measured, cut and fixed correctly, this should not occur.

Sandpaper is available in fine, medium and course sheets. You will probably only need medium and fine. Before you paint or varnish your wood it needs to be as smooth as possible and, once undercoated, it will need re-sanding before top coats are added, as varnish or paint will encourage the grain of the wood to stand up. When sanding after having painted an undercoat, you must use the finest possible sandpaper.

SCREWING AND DRILLING

You will need to screw the frame of the baseboard together and also the spine and the cross-members, plus the actual baseboard. This means that you will have to drill pilot holes in many places and also use a countersink bit as well as a screwdriver. Whilst this

The power screwdriver is almost an essential. With a series of perhaps thirty screws round the top of a baseboard, such a tool is a worthwhile investment. You can use a combined drill/driver, but a specialist screwdriver (with sufficient power) will make life easier.

Sets of drill bits are an essential. The set in the photograph is a general set with masonry, metal and wood bits, but you can purchase sets just for wood.

Spade drill bits are used for drilling out ready for dowels to be fitted. A 25mm (1in) drill will create the right-sized hole for a dowel, but you need to use the 16mm ($^5/_8$ths) bit to take out the slight bump left by the larger drill bit.

The specialist countersunk bit can be purchased separately or is also included in combination drill bit sets. It is handy to have the countersink fitted in a screwdriver and a drill bit in the drill, so that you are not constantly changing between the two. Using a countersink allows the screw head to be sunk below the level surface of the baseboard.

can all be done by hand, most households have an electric drill or a drill/screwdriver combination drill. You will obviously need a range of wood or general purpose drill bits. You will also need to use a 'spade' drill to cut holes in the cross-members and possibly in the frame.

PINNING

If you are using thin plywood cross-members, you will have to use pin nails to hold the wood until the glue has set. Obviously this means that you require a small hammer and a centre punch to sink the heads of the pins into the wood.

A small hammer and centre punch will be needed to pin cross-members into place. The centre punch has a tiny raised edge to stop you slipping off the pin and damaging the woodwork. As these become well used, the edge becomes flat and you need to replace the punch.

CLAMPING

Until the glue has set, you will have to use a variety of clamps to hold items together. Clamps come in a variety of styles and sizes. The quick-release clamp is very useful, especially if working on your own, as other clamps need two hands to operate them. The polycarbon clamp has a quick adjuster but has the disadvantage that it does appear to flex a little when under pressure. The best clamp is the all-metal screw clamp. It is slower but gives a more firm hold than the others. In addition, you will need a series of heavy objects to hold items in place. I tend to use my wife's kitchen weights, but you can use tins of paint or other heavy items.

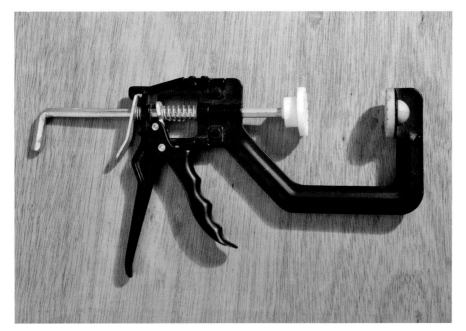

Quick-release clamps are useful when working on your own. For all the other clamps you need two hands for the clamp plus a further hand to hold the items prior to clamping. This clamp allows you to just squeeze the trigger until it is just gripping, make final adjustments and then finally lock into place. Release is achieved by the simple pressing of a lever.

Kitchen weights (or cans of paint) are ideal for holding wood in position – but do remember to put the weights back into the kitchen (clean) when you have finished.

The polycarbonate clamp allows you to push the two clamp faces together, but you have to turn the screw handle to make a firm grip. The moving face also tends to spin round as you tighten and can affect the accuracy of your joint if you are nor careful. When fully tight they do hold the joint but feel a little flexible. Release is achieved by unscrewing the handle.

The all-metal clamp will provide the best hold, but is has no quick release or quick-fitting system, being limited to turning a threaded handle to achieve contact and pressure. You definitely need two hands. I often use one quick-release clamp, and then attach a metal clamp, releasing the first clamp to use on the next joint.

WORKBENCH

Obviously you will need some form of table or, if possible, a workbench to be able to saw or clamp the various parts of your baseboard. If you do not own one, there are several inexpensive workbenches available or even a simple sawhorse can be used.

OTHER ITEMS

It goes without saying that you will need at least pencils, a measure and a ruler, as well as a spirit-level. To score the line of the track on to the baseboard you will require a scalpel or sharp-bladed knife. Later in the process you will require paint brushes and, finally, as well as all through the process, you will need a vacuum cleaner to pick up all the dust, especially after sanding and before painting. To plan and mark out the track you will need a set of 'Tracksetta' guides and obviously lots of PVA glue. I tend to buy PVA in 5-litre cans and dispense it into a more manageable 125ml container for actual use.

BELOW: *Tape-measure with both metric and imperial measurements – an essential tool in the process. A straight steel rule is also valuable for marking out track.*

ABOVE: *The workbench is an invaluable tool. It will clamp odd-shaped wood or long lengths together and it also has the benefit of being able to hold baseboards in a vertical position when you are adding your wiring.*

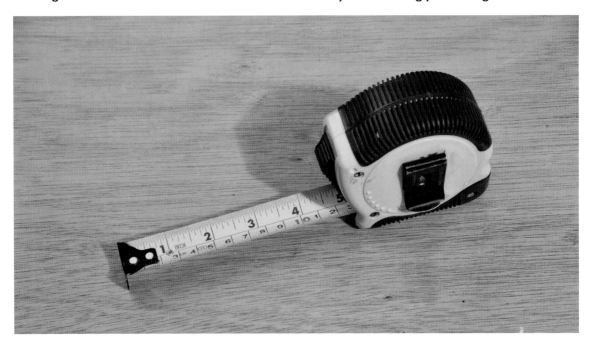

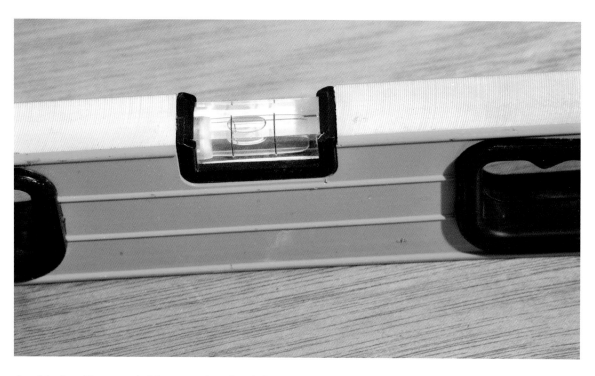

A spirit-level is essential for ensuring that joints are level and that baseboards are level. It can also be used for straight line marking or even as a guide for a jig saw when clamped in the correct position.

Scalpel or Stanley knives are used for marking cut-lines and for marking out tracks on baseboards.

A variety of paint brushes are necessary for spreading glue, putting on undercoats, top gloss coats and for dusting off after sanding.

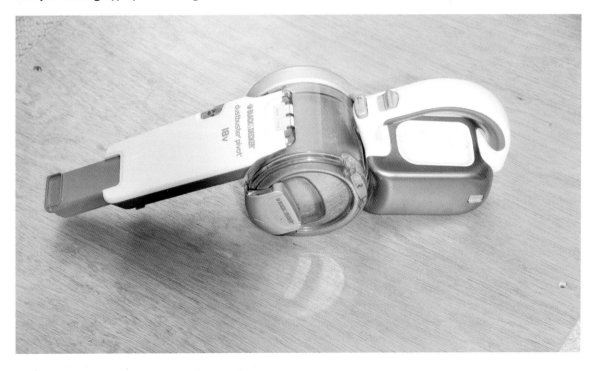

A powerful hand vacuum that can get into a variety of corners is valuable for cleaning boards and work surfaces, prior to painting. A large vacuum is obviously required for floor cleaning.

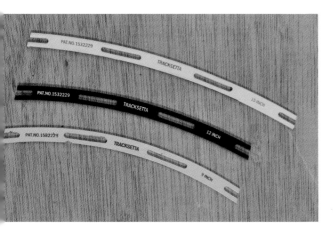

ABOVE: *Tracksetta sets for your gauge are an essential tool for setting out angles of curves. For historic reasons, all track measurements seem to come in imperial radius dimensions.*

RIGHT: *PVA is an essential tool of the railway modeller. The cheaper quality PVA is water soluble, which means it can be dampened after it has hardened to allow track or other removal. For construction of a baseboard, where joints are permanent, it is better to use the more expensive non-soluble version used in the building trade, rather than the soluble version sold in hobby shops and DIY stores. I normally decant from a 5-litre container into a smaller container for actual application.*

Finally, a piece of string, a drawing pin and a pencil are needed to draw out the various radii of the tracks.

PROTECTIVE CLOTHING

It is obviously a matter for each individual as to whether you feel that you want to wear protective clothing, but my advice would be to at least use simple face masks and also wear safety spectacles. Both of these can be purchased for as little as eight pounds. For spectacle wearers, you can purchase Over Specs protective glasses for under two pounds.

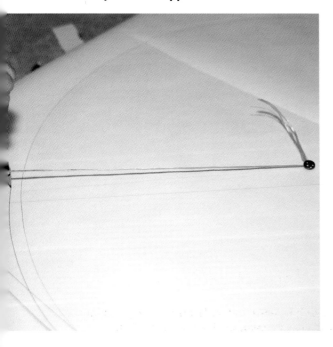

LEFT: *A drawing pin, piece of string and a pencil are almost essential in drawing curves. Set the curvature with a Tracksetta and set the string to the correct length to draw the outer line. Give the string a couple of turns round the pencil until it lines up with the inner track line.*

CHAPTER SEVEN

CONSTRUCTING BASEBOARDS

INTRODUCTION

This chapter aims show you how to construct a variety of different baseboards, starting with the simple, solid wood baseboard and the standard door baseboard, followed by the real construction process of making your baseboard with a softwood frame and plywood board and other variations. It is heavily illustrated at each stage of construction, with a detailed explanation plus hints and tips throughout the construction process.

Previous chapters have already prepared all the ground and it is important that earlier planning steps have been followed. Before you start any construction you should have a full-sized drawing of the layout, so that you can accurately position cross-members and the spine. You should also be clear as to whether the board will have any rises or falls, as this could affect the depth of the frame.

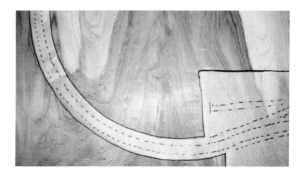

A full-sized plan of part of the planned track extension to 'Pendleton Pit'. This board was covered in cork and the track plan was then laid on top so that excess cork could be removed. The cork was then stuck into place and, when dry, was painted black and then the whole board was sealed with a floor sealer to prevent water ingress. In the centre is a cork base, without paper cut out. This will accommodate the mine track, which is totally separate from the main layout. This paper plan will be removed but form the guide when laying track.

The almost complete flat baseboard constructed in softwood and plywood.

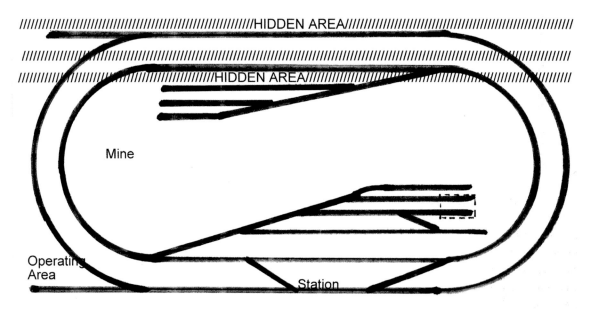

A different plan for a flat baseboard showing areas where the track will be hidden from view.

Plan and baseboard where one track passes under the other.

For the purposes of this book I am constructing several baseboards. The first board will be an extension to my existing two boards for 'Pendleton Pit' and will have a flat surface made to my standard size of 1,100mm (43in) by 700mm (27½in). The softwood frame will run around the edges of the baseboard, so it will be the full 1,100mm (43¼in) by 700mm (27½in). As it is level, it will be constructed in 18mm (¾in) by 44mm (1¾in) softwood, rather than the deeper frame required for the multi-height board.

The first two boards of my current layout have completely flat top surfaces, with the only rise in the ground being at the rear to hide the return tracks of this continuous-run layout. There are two ways that I can tackle the new extension. There will be a single track running round the perimeter of the board to join up with track on the linking board. The first and easiest construction will be on a flat baseboard with all the track that I wish to hide being either behind tightly packed buildings or underneath land that rises, leaving the level track to pass underneath.

The second option is to drop the perimeter track gradually down to a lower level with the ground in the centre rising up slightly to create the height for the perimeter tracks to pass underneath. To achieve this in 1,100mm (43¼in), one track will have to fall as the other one rises. This obviously adds complications to the construction of the baseboard, but this chapter will show how this is achieved. The frame on both of the original boards is made up of 18mm (¾in) x 44mm (1¾in).

THE SOLID WOOD BASEBOARD

Solid wood boards are rarely used. They are heavy to store or move around, costly to make and have similar inflexibilities to the egg-shell door. Sheet timber is expensive and anyone wishing to use a solid board would be well advised to look in second-hand shops or auction houses for old dining-room tables to use as their baseboard. Such tables can be purchased for a song if they are not in good condition.

The only construction work for a solid wood baseboard is to cut it to the selected size and to consider how it is going to be supported. Size calculations are referred to throughout the book and you need to have given full consideration to weight, storage, track radius requirements and the board's support before you cut the wood to the appropriate size. Before you lay the track you need to sand and finish the board as described in Chapter 9.

A solid wooden baseboard.

THE EGG-SHELL (OR HONEYCOMB) DOOR BASEBOARD

The egg-shell baseboard comes in one or two sizes, so you will have to reverse the considerations. Where can I store the layout? Is the layout too heavy? What diameter track layout can I fit on the board? These are all questions to be considered before you choose this option. As with the solid wooden baseboard, this door will need finishing before the track is laid, as described later.

Cheap doors are made with two layers of hardboard with cardboard innards and a thin, wooden frame. These doors used to be easily available, but today even the simplest door is made from a thin timber veneer. Such doors are about the same price as a 1,220mm (48in) x 2,440mm (96in) x 6mm (¼in) plywood sheet. Standard doors are 1,981mm (78in) high and between 760mm (30in) and 838mm (33in) wide. They are rigid and they are light. You cannot screw or pin track to the board – it all has to be glued and you cannot install point motors below the surface. Wiring and motors all have to be on the surface. Doors make an ideal baseboard for the simple home track where points are operated manually and there is a simple track layout, which can be brought out when children want to play with trains.

THE FLAT BASEBOARD

By far the simplest proper baseboard you can construct is the flat baseboard and I suggest that more complicated boards are not tackled until a flat one has been constructed successfully, as this is the basis for most of the other types of baseboard, whether multi-height baseboard, dropped baseboard, layered height baseboard or open-topped baseboard.

THE PLYWOOD FRAME

Plywood frames are usually constructed of 9mm (³⁄₈in) plywood. The process is exactly the same as for softwood frames described above, except that as 9mm (³⁄₈in) plywood is only half the thickness of 18mm (¾in) x44mm (1¾in) softwood, all the measuring and drilling has to be that much more accurate.

Corners, as with softwood, can either be mitred or edge-to-edge (butt) jointed. With plywood you are not restricted by standard depths, as you can cut it or have it cut to any depth you like. I would, however, strongly recommend that you have it professionally cut into strips. This leaves you with the simpler task of just cutting each piece to the appropriate length. There is little point in using plywood unless you need a depth greater than 50mm (2in), as the minimal weight-reduction between plywood and softwood at 44mm (1¾in) is offset by the increase in difficulty of screwing the top to the frame, due to both the narrower width and the plywood construction. Screwing into 9mm (³⁄₈in) plywood requires each hole to be fully pre-drilled and a thin screw, otherwise plywood has a tendency to split away when screwing into the end grain. The biggest factor is the weight. Plywood is approximately 50 per cent of the weight of the thicker softwood. If weight is crucial and you are an accurate worker, then use plywood. However, if weight is crucial it is possible to use a spade drill to bore a series of holes in the softwood frame to reduce the weight, but the amount of weight saved compared with the work required could never be classed as beneficial.

A commercial plywood frame corner joint.
ELITE BASEBOARDS

SOFTWOOD FRAME CONSTRUCTION

As recommended earlier, I have drawn up detailed full-sized track plans for each board on to lining paper and I am clear that my track requirements will fit within that space, whilst not interfering with the frame itself. To make matters easier, I only have four points on the outer line of the flat baseboard plan and only two on the multi-height board plan. The baseboard must be designed around the track plan, not the other way round.

I strongly recommend that, if you are having the sheet plywood professionally cut to the required baseboard top size, you make up and glue the actual frame first. Only when this is complete, have the baseboard and the internal cross-members and the spine cut to the size of your frame. The reason for this is that a professionally cut board will be accurate to the millimetre and in making your frame you could easily be the odd millimetre adrift. On the other hand, if you are cutting the baseboard top yourself, I would cut this first and then cut and make up the frame. It is far easier to remake or trim a piece of frame than it is to make corrections to a baseboard sheet. It is always best to cut framing a thousandth of an inch oversize and trim back when it is found to be too big, when you hold the individual pieces in

position. It is easier to trim back than it is to add to a length. Do not think about fixing the frame pieces together until you are certain that they exactly fit the baseboard sheet.

I cannot stress too strongly the adage 'Measure Twice – Cut Once'.

FRAME CORNERS – BUTT OR MITRE

The frame can be joined at the corners in a variety of ways. My personal choice is to mitre and screw each corner. Using a mitre joint gives approximately 50 per cent more surface contact area than a straight end-to-end joint, and with the aid of a mitre cutting block, is easily achieved. When using a mitre block always use a clamp to hold the wood, as this prevents the wood from moving during the cutting process. Fingers are not usually strong enough to completely fix the wood throughout the cutting process. A mitre join has the advantage of almost automatically making the corners 90-degree square, whereas an end-to-end joint is slightly less reliable. End-to-end joints leave the grain exposed on one of the two pieces of wood and you can only screw into one side, with the point of the screw going into the end grain of the other. Mitre joints allow you to screw into the sides of either length of wood or one screw into

A butt joint glued and screwed. Note it can only be screwed in one direction.

A mitre joint glued and screwed, with one screw from each side making a more rigid joint.

each side. There is no point in trying to accurately measure out the mitre by hand. Any DIY store or hardware shop will sell a simple mitre block and the only other item is a tenon saw. Ensure the length of wood is longer than necessary, then place the wood in the mitre block, as shown, and cut the first mitre.

The next stage is to measure the wood from the mitre along the longest side, and mark carefully the actual length of the wood required. Check your measurements again before sawing and ensure that you have both mitre cuts facing towards each other, not parallel with each other. Make sure that the saw cut is slightly to the right of the distance mark, rather than sawing through the middle of the line, as you have to allow for the thickness of the saw blade. Always cut the longest sides first, as if there is a mistake they can always be cut down to form the shorter sides.

Double check the measurements before cutting the second length. Once complete, put these two sides well out of the way so that you are not tempted to use them for the shorter lengths. Now repeat the process with the two ends of the board so that you end up with the four pieces that form the frame. Push

these all together on a flat surface and check that you have the right size of frame. If it is too long or too wide it is possible to shave thin strips off the offending lengths using the mitre block and tenon saw, but ensure that you take exactly equal amounts off each of the corresponding parallel pieces.

If you plan to use straight end-to-end butt joints, rather than mitres, still follow the instructions using the 90-degree cut on the mitre block, as opposed to the 45-degree cut. All the other instructions are the same.

Do not sand them down at this stage.

CONSTRUCTING MULTIPLE BOARD FRAMES AND PREPARING FOR DOWELS

If you are making a layout that has more than one board, or you are adding to an existing layout, it is essential that you fix furniture maker's joint dowels at this stage. Once you have the top of the baseboard fitted or, worse still, the cross-members and spine fitted, it is not possible to fit a normal drill and obtain an exactly parallel set of holes for the dowels. If you are making two or more boards, clamp each

A multiple set of baseboards ready for track laying.

Lines marked on end boards to ensure a complete match between the two ends.

Drilling the pilot holes for dowels. Note the two pieces clamped together to ensure accuracy. An alternative is to use a simple jig.

set of end boards together but ensure that they are in exact register and that the mitres are chamfered inwards, so that the two external faces of the frame are face-to-face. Put two pencil lines across the top but to one side. By matching these lines up you will ensure that you have the right pieces joining together and that they are both the right way up.

If you are joining a new board to an old layout you have to take greater care in ensuring that they are both accurately lined up. In my case, the end frames of the rise and fall baseboard are different depths to the baseboard fitted to the existing layout. You must double check several times that they are both clamped in exactly the correct position before drilling. Once drilled and the dowel installed there is no adjustment.

To install dowels, first drill a hole through both end panels with a 2mm ($1/20$in) (or similar sized) drill bit. The dowels need to be fitted about 1/6th of the way in from the sides to ensure that the boards marry up exactly across the whole width. If you are going to fasten the two boards together with bolts, you also need to drill two holes using a 10mm ($3/10$in) bit. These holes need to be about one third of the way in from the sides. There are other ways of joining boards that do not require drilling at this stage. The main alternative is the toggle latch (see Chapter 10).

Once the pilot holes for the dowels have been drilled and other holes (if bolting the units together), you can undo the clamps and separate the two ends. Clearly mark the two faces that will come into contact with each other when complete. These boards will have an off-centre mark on the top and be clearly marked that they are the outer sides of the frame, and also a frame number if you are producing more than two boards. In this way there is little possibility of drilling the wrong side or in the wrong position.

On the outer faces of each end use a flat (or spade) 25mm bit. You must keep the drill at 90 degrees to the wood and drill out just sufficient to fit the dowel plate into the wood, so that the front face is level with the surface of the wood. If you drill too deeply, the point of the dowel will not completely go home into the female end of the dowel. If you do not drill deeply enough, the two pieces of wood will be

Marking the outer face of the end to ensure that you do not fit the dowel on the wrong side.

The point of a spade drill bit to be inserted into the pilot hole to ensure both ends are lined up correctly. Note that the 'spade' part of the drill bit is taller on the outside than in the centre. The hole it cuts out is therefore slightly humped.

A partly drilled hole for the dowel. Drilling stops just before the dowel is level with the wood surface.

A dowel, slightly above the surface level and also rocking on the small 'hump' left by the 25mm (1in) drill bit.

A 16mm (⁵⁄₈in) drill bit removes sufficient of the 'hump'.

kept slightly proud of each other. One advantage of using plywood is that you can see whether you are drilling accurately, as you need to ensure that you are removing the different layers of wooden laminate evenly, as the wood will probably change either colour or texture with each layer. The spade drill is not totally flat and it cuts minimally deeper on the outside edge than in the centre. It is important that you drill just sufficient to leave the foot of the dowel minimally protruding from the surface of the wood. Then, using a 16mm spade drill, carefully remove the slightly higher centre, so that the dowel sits flat and level. (The remaining slight rise at the very centre will be levelled out when the screws are inserted and the wood compressed.)

The hole you have drilled is 25mm (1in) diameter and the dowel is 24mm, so there is a little slack; however, the dowel needs to be in exactly the right place. Fix both the male dowels with only one of the three screws, and make sure they are tight. The wood behind the centre of the female dowel needs to be enlarged to accommodate the male dowel. Use an 8mm (⁵⁄₈in) drill bit to bore this hole. The hole can go all the way through, or it can be just sufficient to take the depth of the male end of the dowel

Enlarging the hole behind the female dowel to allow unobstructed access for the male dowel.

Male dowel with one of its three screws being tightened into place following verification of the correct alignment. The female dowel with three screws fixed.

(approximately 12mm/½in deep). Then fit the screws to tightly hold the female ends of each dowel. Push the two wooden ends together and ensure that they line up exactly as you want, ensuring that the tops are level. Carefully ease the two wooden ends apart and, without moving them in their holes, screw up another screw on the male dowels. Once again clamp them together to ensure that they line up correctly, then carefully separate and screw up the remaining screws on the male dowels. If for some reason they do not exactly line up the two surfaces, you can adjust them by loosening one set of screws and turning the dowel to give you fresh wood to try again.

If you are fitting bolts, you need to insert a metal rod in each piece of wood, otherwise, over time, the hole will become slack. The hole you have drilled will be just too tight for the rod, so it will have to be hammered home. Once again, clamp both pieces of end panel together with the dowels in place. Cut the 10mm (³/₁₀in) rod into lengths slightly shorter than the width of the frame (in this case less than 18mm/¾in). Coat the wooden hole with UHU or a similar glue to bind the metal to the wood, then, resting the cut rod on the hole, insert an M8 bolt through the rod and both pieces of wood. Use the

Cutting a length off the rod to fit in the end plate to ensure continued accuracy of the joining bolt.

Using a spare bolt to knock home the glued piece of rod.

Installing the rod in the second end plate by passing the bolt through the end plate with its rod in place and knocking the new piece of rod using the bolt as a guide.

shaft of the bolt to guide the rod and the bolt head as the 'punch' to drive the rod home. Once complete, remove the bolt and repeat on the other face. This will ensure that both rods are installed correctly and that they line up with the bolt, at the same time as the dowels are correctly aligning the ends.

If you are fitting a different jointing system, such as toggle clamps (a preferred option), this latter paragraph does not apply.

You can now unclamp the two ends and ensure that you keep them as a pair.

If you want to keep the weight of the baseboard to an absolute minimum, now is the time to bore a series of holes along each side and a couple in each end. (See note earlier in this chapter on the effort-for-gain benefits.) Carefully mark out the centre line of the wood and then mark out a series of equally spaced points about 75mm (3in) apart. Leave 150mm (6in) at each end to allow for the fitting of the leg supports. Using a 25mm (1in) flat or spade bit, bore a hole until the point of the drill appears on the other side. Turn the wood over and drill through the rest of the way until the wooden 'plug' is removed. (If you only drill from one side, the drill will split pieces of wood on the reverse side as it makes its way though.) It is important to stop drilling and turn over fairly

A side frame marked out ready for drilling in order to reduce weight.

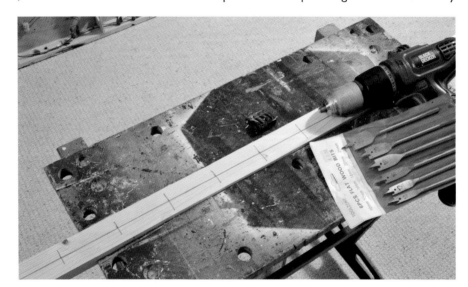

Drilling out the side frame.

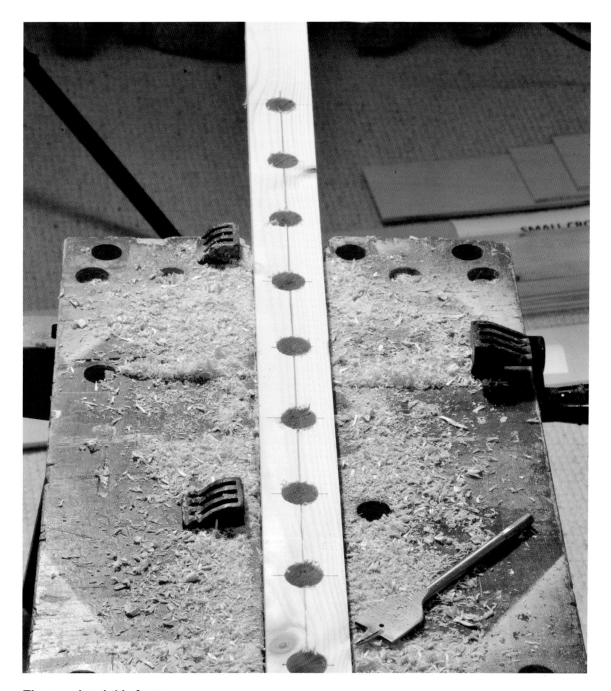

The completed side frame.

soon after the bit's pilot hole has come through to the far side. The deeper you drill, the wider the pilot hole becomes and the less accurate will be the final, completed hole. I always leave the public (or viewing) side without holes to permit the attachment of a curtain with a Velcro strip. An alternative, especially when drilling plywood, is to clamp a waste piece of wood to the rear of the main piece and drill all the way through. In most cases this will prevent the rear of the main piece of wood from splintering.

Two plywood cross-members with their backing sheet. Note that only the backing sheet of plywood has splinter damage.

MAKING UP THE FRAME

The next task is to make up the frame. If you have mitred the joints, you need to clamp them together and ensure that they are flat. The best way is to have a sheet of wood that you know is square, place a piece of paper over one corner and then align the first side so that it is exactly in line with the side and comes exactly to the corner. Using at least one clamp, fasten the side to the piece of wood. Taking the other side, drill a couple of pilot holes ready for screws and use the countersink bit to ensure that the screws will fit flush. Smear glue on both mitres and bring the two pieces together. Clamp them both in position, but have one clamp extremely tight and the other clamp permitting slight movement. The piece with movement must be the piece with the screws. Check alignment with a set square. Tighten up both screws and then tighten the clamp. Ideally, leave for a while for the PVA glue to set or at least begin to harden.

Undo the clamps and peel off the paper. The paper stops the glue making a bond with the sheet of wood. Repeat the process with the other two sides to create the opposite corner. Again, using the wood as a template, join the four sides together. This should

Two mitred sides and two mitred ends.

ABOVE: *The end is screwed up tight and then clamped until dry.*

LEFT: *One side firmly clamped on to paper covered plywood with a guaranteed 90-degree corner. The end is clamped in place.*

holes along the sides of the frame are best sanded with sandpaper wrapped round a finger.

Instead of using a tenon saw and a mitre board, you could use a chop saw. These saws are very accurate and will cut an excellent mitre. Before you cut, make sure the saw is set to 45 degrees and that, if it is a compound chop saw, the blade is also set in the vertical position. Usually if you pick compound saws up to put them on a workbench, the blade will move slightly out of vertical because the grab handle is not exactly at the centre of balance. A compound chop saw will cut at any angle in both directions – vertically and horizontally – and it is vital in constructing a frame that the saw blade is vertical to the base and the other is 45 degrees to the cutting surface. Remember to allow for the thickness of the saw cut when positioning the saw blade.

The above frame construction processes apply to a flat-topped baseboard, a multi-level baseboard or an open baseboard, a dropped baseboard or a folding baseboard.

result in your completed frame, which is not only rectangular with 90-degree corners, but it will lay flat when put on a flat surface. Do not worry at this stage if it is slightly out of square as this can be corrected.

Leave the frame on a flat surface to hard dry, then sand down all the surfaces and the corners, either with a hand sander or a detail or plate sander. The

A mitre board and tenon saw cutting a mitre.

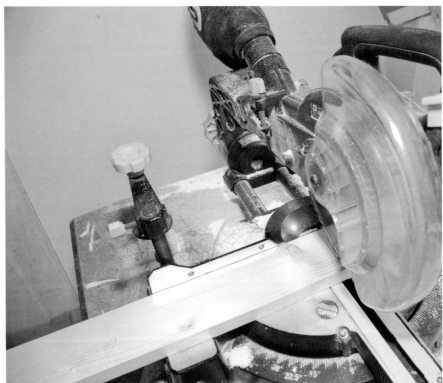

A chop saw cutting a 90-degree section of frame side. This saw can easily be set to cut mitre joints.

THE BASEBOARD TOP

There are several materials used for baseboard tops. Historically, most modellers used to use Sundela board. Its advantages are that track pins can be easily tapped into the board and it absorbs noise better than other materials. The disadvantages are that in changing temperature and humidity situations it has a tendency to warp. It is also relatively heavy and the ends need to have some protection, otherwise corners and edges can easily break away.

In a few cases MDF has taken over as a preferred material. It is cheaper than Sundela and also cheaper than plywood, but it has the disadvantages that it too will warp under different humidity and temperature conditions, it is quite heavy and track pins need to have the MDF drilled, as you cannot easily knock them in. It also creates an appalling amount of dust when it is cut.

Common practice today is to use 3.6mm ($^1/_{16}$in) or 6mm ($^1/_4$in) exterior quality plywood (slightly thicker if you are dealing with 'O' gauge). This has the advantage that it is light, almost waterproof and, when fixed with cross-members, does not warp. Its

one big disadvantage is that it is noisy – it will 'drum' as trains pass over it. This is usually overcome to some extent by laying the track on a cork sheet. It also requires holes to be drilled for track pins.

There is nothing to stop you building the baseboard of much thicker materials but there is almost no gain in required strength. Making everything thicker results in the board being more cumbersome to move around and there is a tremendous increase in weight.

Plywood of 3.6mm ($^1/_{16}$in) thick only comes in widths of 606mm (24in) or less, but 6mm ($^1/_4$in) plywood comes in a variety of sizes from 606mm (24in) x 1,220mm (48in), 607mm (24in) x 1,829mm (72in) and 1,220mm (48in) x 2,440 (96in). It also comes in 9mm ($^3/_8$in), 12mm ($^1/_2$in) and 18mm ($^3/_4$in) thicknesses. The size you require will depend on the size of your layout. If you are planning an end-to-end layout, you will probably not need a top wider than 606mm (24in), but as mine is a continuous layout I need it to be 700mm (27$^1/_2$in) wide. My only choice is the 1,220mm (48in) x 2,440mm (96in) sheet. Whilst smaller sizes will fit in most cars, such a sheet obvi-

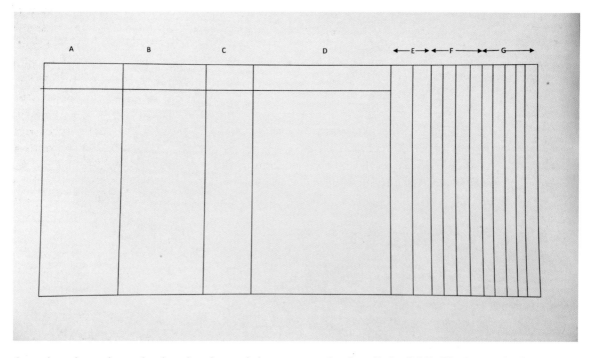

A cutting plan prior to having the plywood sheet cut professionally by B&Q. The letters indicate the cutting sequence.

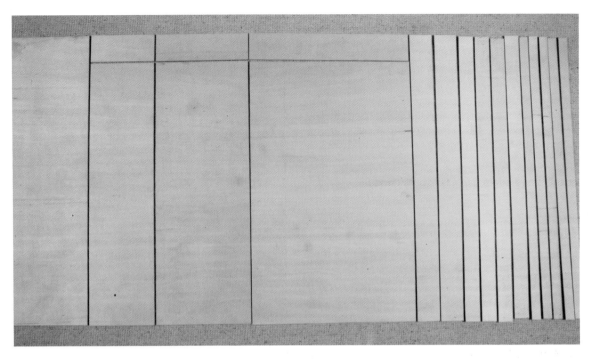

The actual plywood sheet as cut and laid out as previously planned.

ously will not. I have a B&Q store not too far away that offers a cutting service and I would recommend anyone to make use of any company offering such a facility. Most places will make several cuts for free, but check before you commit. Not only do you get the wood cut square, without many chips being broken off by the saw, but you end up with it being easily transportable in a car and exactly the right size to fit your frame (if you have measured correctly).

It is not just a matter of working out the sizes of plywood that you want, but working out the best way of achieving this from the smallest piece of wood and then sorting out a cutting sequence. The big commercial saw machines stand the wood on its side and then cut vertically for best results. They usually cut from the right-hand side and it is possible to obtain thin slices of plywood for the cross-members and spine, if you have these cut whilst there is still a reasonable amount of remaining wood for the wood clamp attached to the saw to grip. Remember that the blade will take about 2mm ($^{1}/_{20}$in) from the wood, so you need to allow for this by leaving the piece resulting from this last cut a little flexible in its size.

The plan I have drawn up for my cutting requirements covers both the flat baseboard and most of the materials for the multi-level baseboard, as this will be the best use for a stock size of 6mm plywood sheet. The first five cuts will be 40mm (1½in) wide each. These will form the cross-members and spine. The next four will be 65mm (2½in) (the cross-members and spine for the deeper board). I will make the short cuts for the required lengths at home with a chop saw. The two pieces, each 200mm (8in), will form the up and down gradients. Next is the flat baseboard, 1,100mm (43in) by 700mm (27½in). The two pieces, 1,100mm (43in) by 280mm (11in) and 1,100mm (43in) by 400mm (15¾in), will form two of the different levels on the variable-height board. This single sheet of 2,440mm by 1,220mm by 6mm plywood will provide me with all I need to make up the first baseboard, plus the bulk of a second baseboard. As this baseboard will form part of an exhibition layout, the remaining sheet, measuring just less than 400mm (15¾in) by 1,100mm (43in), will be used to form a front slope that will carry printed information about the layout and the West Wiltshire

Model Railway Circle, at the same time as keeping small hands away from the tracks and rolling stock. This unit just bolts on to the main baseboard when at the exhibition.

As soon as you get your cut plywood home, lay it flat on the floor so that it does not twist. It will have been in a wood store or warehouse, where both temperature and humidity are different than in a house or garage. To ensure it does not twist, also place some weights on top of the flat sheets – paint cans are ideal. Leave the sheets for a few days to acclimatize to their new conditions before starting work on them.

When you are ready, take a sheet and marry it up to the frame you have made and check that it fits. As long as it is the correct size, even if the frame is not completely rectangular, you can proceed to the next stage. Bore a series of 2mm ($^1/_{20}$in) or smaller pilot holes around the top edge of the baseboard sheet, about 75mm (3in) apart, and then use a countersink bit to countersink each hole. Before you apply PVA glue, ensure that you have enough screws to complete the task, as the baseboard top needs to be completely secured before the glue dries.

Lay the frame on a solid, flat surface and spread PVA glue on the top edge. Carefully locate the plywood baseboard on the top of the frame, adjusting it slightly until it is flush on one side and the two ends align correctly at the bottom corners. Do not worry if the top corners are not 100 per cent correctly aligned at this stage.

Screw home one screw in each of the two bottom corners and, if the softwood frame is slightly bowed, you can pull it in line before inserting the centre screw. As soon as it is flush, either hold it or clamp it in position and insert a screw in the centre. Now is the time to ease the frame into its final shape to fit exactly with the baseboard in all four corners. With one side fixed with three screws, push the frame into shape to match the baseboard top. As soon as you have it square, insert three more screws on the opposite side and then gradually go round inserting alternate screws. Finally, continue filling in with the remaining screws. This will pull the baseboard evenly in contact with the frame.

Boring pilot holes in the baseboard top prior to fitting.

*Countersinking
each hole.*

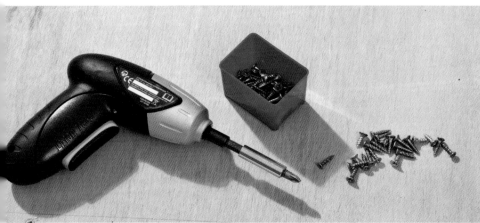

*Ensure you have a
screwdriver (with
the battery fully
charged) and the
screws prior to
gluing.*

Gluing the frame.

Wipe away all excess PVA glue from both the outside and inside of the frame and baseboard, and finish with a damp rag. Lay face up on newspaper on a totally flat surface. Ideally, put weights on each corner and in the centre of the baseboard and leave to dry overnight.

The following day, remove the weights and peel off any newspaper that has stuck. (If it does not come off cleanly, dampen it with warm water – this will soften the PVA and the paper can then be easily removed.) If you have to dampen it, allow it to dry before proceeding.

Lining up the corners on one side and inserting a screw in each corner of one side and one in the middle.

Pushing the frame to line up exactly with the baseboard top.

The next stage is to sand both the back and front of the board and all the sides and edges. You will probably have to use a medium grade at first, but always finish off with a fine grade. Wipe the whole board with a damp cloth to remove any remaining sanded wood particles. It is best to do the sanding at this stage, before you install the cross-members and spine, as it is much easier to sand down the underneath without the obstruction of the cross-members and spine.

Weighting the board down after gluing.

Using a detail sander to smooth the underneath before the cross-members are added.

CROSS-MEMBERS

The next stage is to install the cross-members. First, you need to lay your full-sized plan on the layout and mark where point motors and other items that could interfere with cross-members are located. For example, I will be installing pit head gear and this will hopefully be motorized. The last thing I want is either the spine or a cross-member being in line with the mechanics of the mine.

Remember that, as you are working on the reverse of the baseboard, you need to have your plan upside down as well. If you have drawn your track plan with a felt-tipped pen on lining paper or banqueting paper, you will be able to see the track plan through the paper. You do not need the detail, only sufficient to be able to set out the cross-members and the spine. Once all the key points are marked, work out where you would ideally locate the cross-members, usually about 300mm (12in) apart, and adjust the position of any that are close to points or other obstructions. Clearly mark these positions on the underside of the board with a felt-tip marker so that you do not use the wrong marks. Assuming that you have had your cross-members cut when having your baseboard sheet cut, and using either a chop saw or the 90-degree position on a mitre board and tenon saw, cut the 6mm (¼in) plywood cross-members to make a snug fit between the two sides. Bore very fine holes in the sides to correspond with each cross-member and insert fine pin nails so that the nail points are just protruding from each of the sides.

Wires are likely to have to pass through these cross-members and before installing you need to bore a series of holes to accommodate the wires. These holes can be made with a simple drill of about 16mm or with a spade drill. In either case you will be able to cut all of the cross-members at the same time. Place a spare solid piece of wood behind them and clamp all the cross-members to it. In making the holes this way you will have few splinters at the back of each cross-member. The same process applies for the spine pieces. If you have not already done so, sand down the cross-members so that they are free of any saw bits before gluing into place.

Place a layer of PVA glue along the line you have drawn on the underside of the baseboard and up the sides over the nails. (If you put the glue on the cross-member you will loose a percentage of it on to the back of the baseboard as you flex the cross-member when you push it into position.) Taking the cross-member, push it into the slightly protruding pin nails on one side and bend it into a slight bow whilst bringing the other end to make contact with the pin nails on the other side. Ensure that the pins are in the centre of the 6mm (¼in) plywood and that the whole length of the inner edge is in contact with the underside of the baseboard. Press down as hard as possible. Knock home the pin nails with a hammer and use a centre punch to sink them slightly into the wood. I usually have a couple of blocks of wood alongside the cross-member and balance tins of paint between the cross-member and the blocks of wood to hold it firmly in contact with the underside of the baseboard top until set. I usually also add a little more PVA along each side to complete the join and leave until dry. Repeat the process with the remaining cross-members. The other alternative is to use clamps to maintain contact between the spine and the underside of the baseboard.

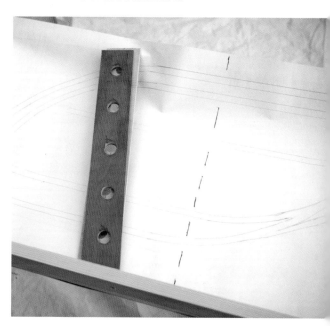

Using the plan to determine the position of the cross-members in relation to track and points.

Marking out the length of the cross-members against the actual frame.

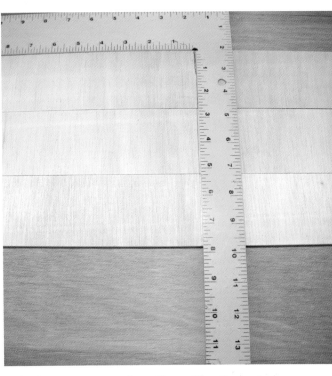

Using a set square to draw the cutting line.

Testing the 'snugness' of the fit before proceeding.

The position line of the cross-member and the pins in the side frame.

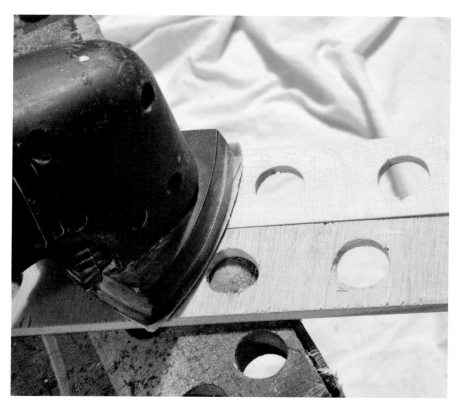

Having cut holes for wires, etc., to pass through, the cross-members need to be sanded down.

The holes are best cleaned with a finger wrapped in sandpaper.

PVA glue along the position line for the cross-member.

The cross-member pushed into the two pins of the frame and slotted into the correct position on the baseboard.

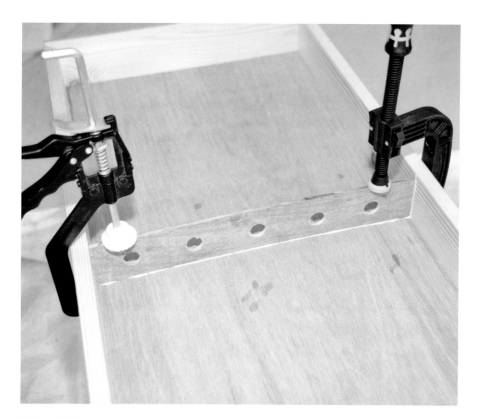

The cross-member held down with clamps until dry.

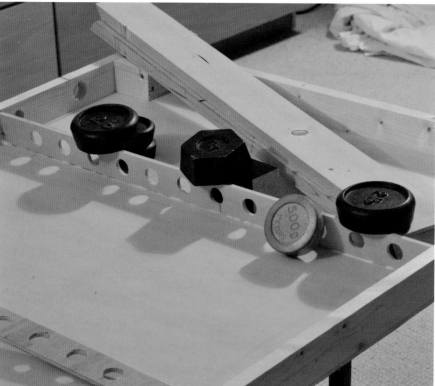

An alternative method of holding the cross-member with wood and weights.

The final stage is to install the spine. With the cross-members fixed in place, the spine has to be made up of several pieces, fitted between the end panels and the various cross-members. Cut each section carefully so that they are a tight fit. Put pin nails into the end panels, as before, but in the inter-mediate joints, glue is sufficient. Once dry, add a little more glue to make sure of a good fix. If you feel a little unsure about the quality of your joints, you can add sections of quarter-round and glue them into place. A simple clamp will hold these tight until the glue dries. Lay the whole board flat again and put weights on to each section of the spine until hard dry.

The basic construction of your flat-topped base-board is now almost complete. With your track plan attached to the top of the baseboard, you need to transfer your track detail to the actual board. The best way is to take a scalpel or very sharp cutting blade and cut along the lines of the track marked out on the paper. You need to cut deeply in order to score the wood underneath. Not only will this leave you with a cut-out of the track, but also a baseboard that has been scored with the track layout. Take a felt-tipped pen and draw along the score lines. The pen will easily follow the slight cut in the wood – a slight wobble does not matter as it is only a guide as to the track plan.

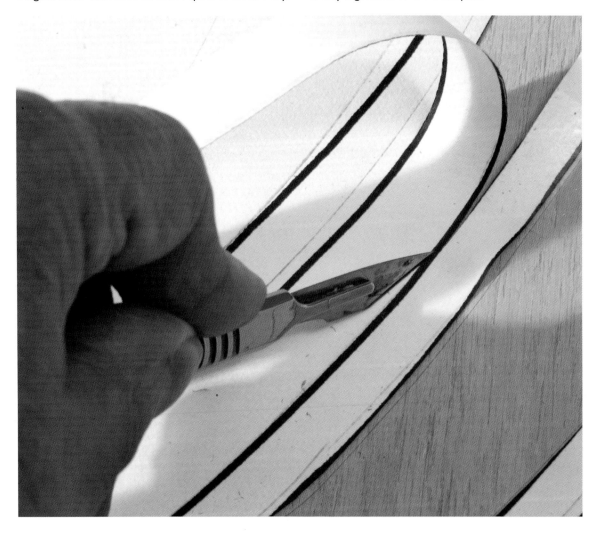

Using a scalpel to mark out the track position on the baseboard. Cutting both removed the excess paper and scored the baseboard top.

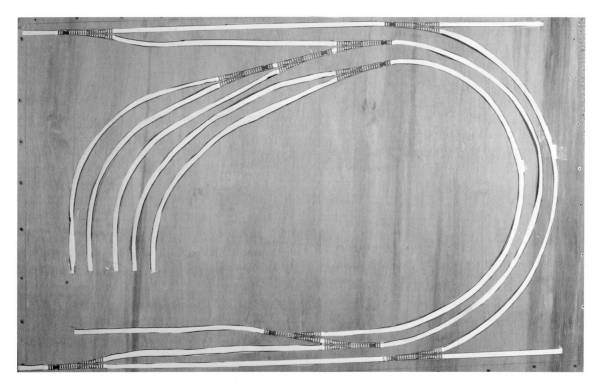

The remaining paper plan on the scored baseboard top.

Inking in the scored lines of the track.

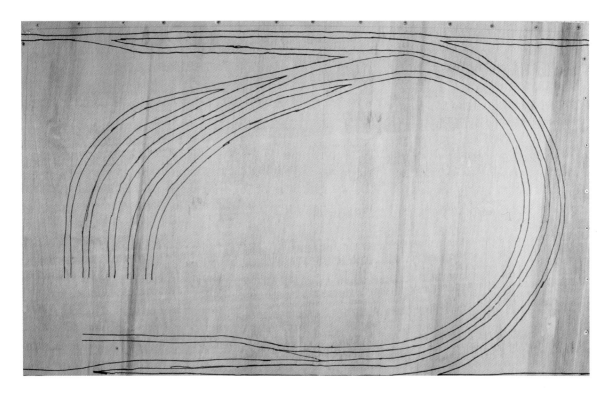

The inked in plan transferred to the baseboard.

THE BASEBOARD WITH VARIED HEIGHT TRACKS

One of the other boards being produced for this part of the book will be an alternative extension to my 'N'-gauge layout 'Pendleton Pit'. This new board will extend the length of the layout by a further 1,200mm (47¼in).

GRADIENTS

As I have said, the track in part is going to rise and, more importantly, fall. The maximum recommended gradient for track is 1:50, so in a length of 900mm (35½in) (allowing for a small level area just after the board join) the maximum height gain is about 18mm (¾in). For one track to pass under another there needs to be a minimum of 32mm (1¼in) clearance between the track and the upper ground level in 'N' gauge, so one track has to go up and one go down. Even then, I need to allow for the thickness of the board supporting the upper track, so it can only just

be achieved. In fact the gradient will be very slightly greater on the downward slope than it will be on the upward slope, as trains and locos will cope with a greater downward slope better than they will a rising slope. This will allow me slightly greater clearance than space really allows, whilst not taxing locos on the 'up' slope.

In this situation working out the exact design in your head is somewhat difficult and to make it easier I always find it simpler to make up a card mock-up. Obviously the frame will still run round the outside of the baseboard, so it will be the full 1,200mm (47¼in) by 750mm (29½in). However, because there is a fall in the track at one end, the frame will have to be deeper. It would be possible to gradually increase the depth from one end to the other by cutting the two sides with a slight diagonal dropping from 44mm (1¾in) to the required 69mm (2¾in) depth, but it is far easier to make the frame in 18mm (¾in) by 69mm (2¾in) all round and to drop the perimeter track almost to the base level of the frame, at the same time as lifting the internal tracks above the height of the frame. Where the two boards join together, the tops of the frames are at the same height.

Making a multi-height board is far more challenging and time-consuming. I can only reiterate that, ideally, you should construct a flat baseboard before attempting boards with more than one level.

The concept was that there was to be a continuous track running round the perimeter, dropping from the standard level to pass underneath the upper track at the far end. This upper track was to be a terminus station. This was roughly sketched out but the next task was to work out the mathematics of the slope required. First, there needs to be a level section following the join and then a point to allow traffic to pass on to the upper or lower baseboard. The minimum length for this is 150mm (6in). The curved track at the lower level needs to be level for 200mm (8in). With a drop of 17mm (¾in) required to allow clearance for my 'N'-gauge locos, the length required for the slope to create a gradient of 1:50 is 850mm (33½in). Adding the three measurements of

850mm (33½in), 150mm (6in) and 200mm (8in) gives an overall baseboard length of 1,200mm (47¼in). As clearance required for one track to pass under another is 34mm (1½in), the upper surface has to rise by 17mm (¾in). It is essential that this geometry is calculated before any work commences. It is only at this stage that a track plan can be produced to full scale.

To be sure I have the concept worked out I always make a cardboard mock-up at 25 per cent of the full size: 190mm (7½in) x 300mm (12in). I use artist's mountboard to make sample boards, as it is both rigid enough and easy to cut. Making a model to scale is far quicker, easier to adjust and cheaper than working in plywood. Making the model will show up all the problems that may occur and will also give you a guide as to possible material requirements.

As I have said, the outer frame for this baseboard will be constructed in 18mm (¾in) by 69mm (2¾in) softwood and this is made up in exactly the same way as the flat baseboard. The dowels are attached and the joining bolt holes are drilled before the board is

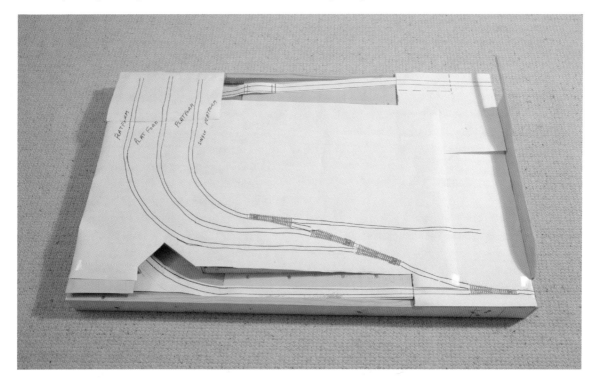

Full-scale plan laid on the finished baseboard.

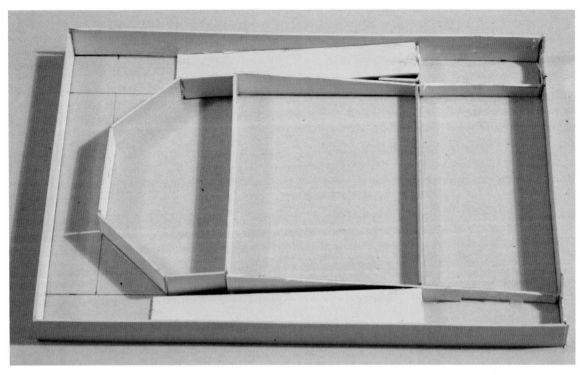

Cardboard mock-up of baseboard to check calculations.

Practical clearance test once baseboard frame is completed – a coach on temporary track to ensure it passes under the top of the supports for the upper baseboard.

constructed, so follow the instructions for dowels and bolts in the flat baseboard section. Also lay some track and add a coach to check clearances, as soon as the frame is made.

In my case this board will butt up to an existing board with scenery and this landscape will have to be matched with an end support. I have found that the best system is to draw out the contour of the scenery on to 6mm (¼in) plywood, cut this to shape, then screw and glue it to the end before cutting the final dowel and bolt holes. This partly made frame and baseboard is then checked by fitting to the existing baseboard to ensure that everything lines up perfectly.

With this sort of baseboard you still need to make up the outer frame first. As with a standard flat baseboard, you need to have at least a small, level piece of baseboard that will join up to the existing flat top to give a level join between boards, prior to starting the different slopes to vary the height. Using the pre-prepared track plan, and the initial calculations, I was able to calculate the size of board needed to create the flat area prior to having the large sheet cut to size.

Having made the frame, as described earlier, the next task is to fit this level area. This baseboard top is drilled, countersunk, glued and screwed in exactly the same way as for a flat baseboard, except that it only covers part of the frame.

Once you have this baseboard top in place, you can begin to construct the lower level baseboard. This will also stretch across the whole width of the frame, but will only provide a base for the part of the track that is at the lowest level. Although I had the length cut out of the big 2,440mm (96in) by 1,220mm (48in) sheet, I needed to cut the width myself. I could have used a circular saw, but this tends to pull off parts of the plywood, leaving a slightly jagged finish. I prefer to use a jig saw with an extremely fine blade. To keep it in line, I position the saw blade on the line and then clamp a length of wood parallel to the line to be cut but in line with the side of the jig saw. By ensuring that the saw base is kept in contact with the wooden guide, it is possible to cut a perfectly straight line. In using a jig saw, the blade cuts on the up stroke

Drilling for dowels.

Dowel ready for insertion.

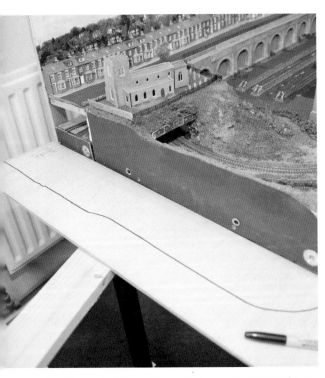

End board with outline of the end scenery from main board.

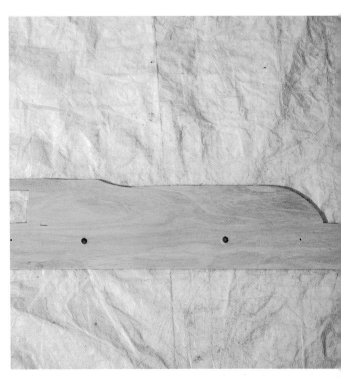

Cut end board and dowel hole pilot holes ready for drilling.

End board fitted and new board linked to master board of the model layout.

The top baseboard glued and screwed into place.

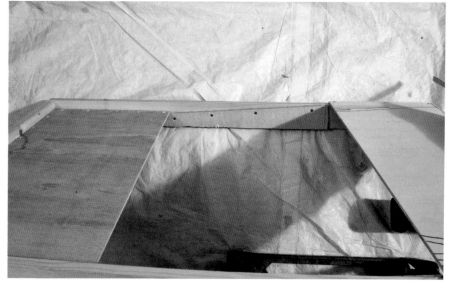

The lower baseboard has to fit inside the frame and needs cutting. A strip of wood is clamped to the board to be cut so that the plate of the jig saw can be held in a straight line.

The bottom baseboard fitted on top of the sub-frame 40mm (1½in) from the bottom of the main frame.

and thus any bits that are chipped out are to be found on the top side. To achieve the best results, either cut from the underneath or add a second spare piece of plywood to supply support when cutting. A circular saw works in the exact opposite way, therefore the prime side should always be on top.

The top of the lower baseboard needs to be located at 17mm (¾in) from the underside of the top baseboard. To achieve this with a 6mm (¼in)

baseboard, you need to glue a sub-frame and cross-members 45mm (1¾in) from the bottom of the frame and then glue the lower level baseboard to the top of this sub-frame. The lower level baseboard will be cut to 664mm (26¼in) to fit inside the 700mm (27½in) external width of the frame (700mm/27½in less twice the frame thickness of 18mm/¾in = 664mm/27¼in and 200mm/8in long). This will help to make sure that the complete frame is exactly square.

You now have a frame with two full-width baseboard tops, one is on the top and only a short length, the other is half-way down the frame at the other end, but both only stretch part of the length of the frame.

The track plan for this baseboard is similar to the flat baseboard. There is a track running round the outside, but this drops down from normal baseboard height, whilst the centre part is raised by a similar amount. This permits the lower track to lie underneath and hidden from the upper layer. On to this lower baseboard, having used the full-sized track plan to mark out the track, you need to install a series of roof supports to hold the upper level. These need to be 34mm (1½in) in height. From the model and the track plan you will be able to determine the positioning of the basic inner frames to support this roof/upper baseboard. Measure your various lengths of wood and cut them to size, making sure that, where it is possible, they stretch to the sides of the frame.

Cut out track plan to determine length and position of upper roof supports.

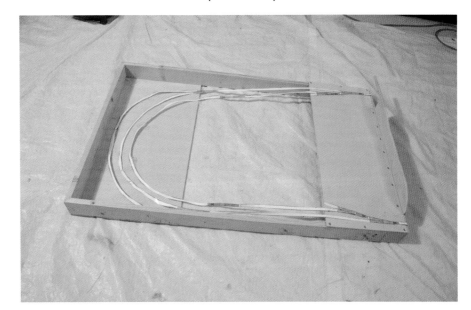

Roof supports glued into place.

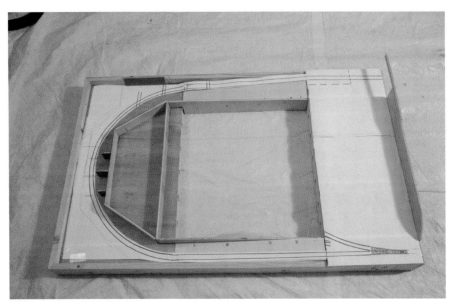

Having drawn out the plan of the outer circuit and the inner area tracks, the next stage is to construct slopes between the upper and lower baseboards. To form the slopes, you have cut four lengths of wood that will be level with the frame at the bottom but vary on the top from the full 69mm (2¾in), down to 45mm (1¾in). Two of these are glued directly to the frame and the ends are glued to the cross-member of both the upper and lower baseboard ends. The remaining two slopes are glued parallel to the frame to form the inner walls of the slopes between the two levels. (These sloping walls cannot be cut by a professional cutting service, as they are not horizontal or vertical, so they have to be cut by you.) They are fixed to the cross-members at the ends of the upper baseboard top at one end and the lower baseboard top at the other. To the top of these sloping inner walls, the track boards can be attached.

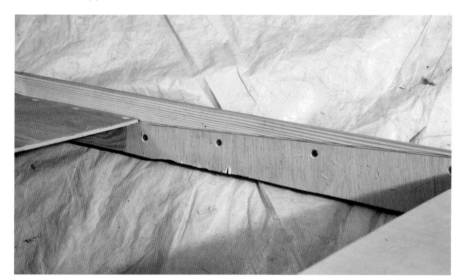

The support for the slope between the two levels showing the lower level baseboard in place.

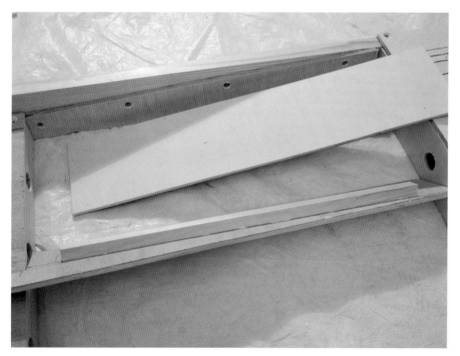

The boards to support the inside of the slope and the slopes themselves are cut to size.

You now need to create a frame that will support the upward slope of the inner baseboard. This is most easily achieved by fixing 18mm (¾in) framing softwood to the inner side of the slope between the underside of the level baseboard end up to the level of the supports fitted to the lower baseboard at the other end. The upper baseboard is best made from 3.6mm (¹/₁₆in) plywood, as you can create a slight curve between the 1:50 slope and the level top with this thickness. Taking your full-sized plan, mark out the track, as previously described, before cutting, gluing and finally screwing it to the inner frame. It will take a little pressure to create the curve but, once screwed and glued, it will remain in place. To ensure firm contact of this flexed plywood, I use heavy weights (2 x 10-litre paint cans in this case).

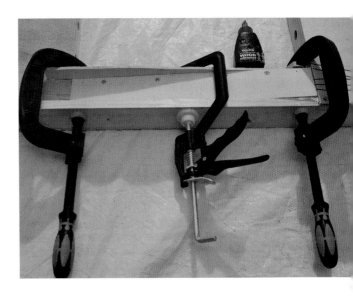

The completed slope.

The upturned baseboard showing the softwood rails to support the upper baseboard.

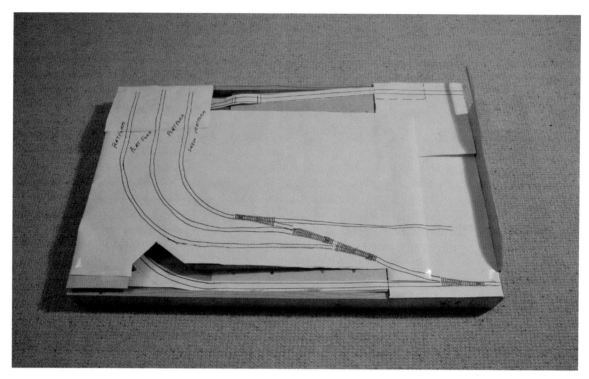

The upper baseboard resting in place with the track plan added, but before removal of the cut-away.

The upper baseboard showing the track markings. The slope to the lower level is also visible.

The one major problem with one track passing under another at a lower level is access. Provision for access needs to be made, otherwise it is almost guaranteed that this is where trains will derail or stop. I have created a removable section at the far end of the higher level and I designed the layout so that a platform will sit on top of most of the removable section with only a small piece of end track being included in the area to be removed.

Track drawn on baseboard with cut-away section to allow access to lower level.

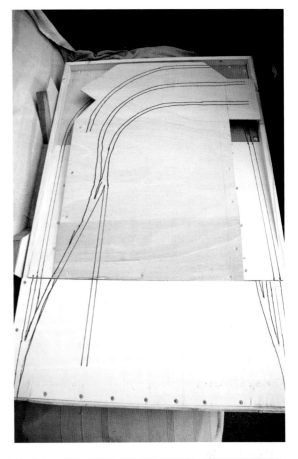

The cut-away in place prior to fitting the top board.

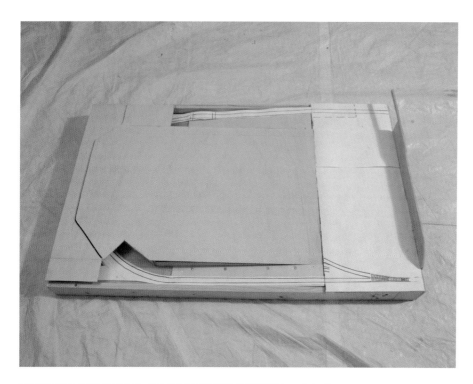

Cut-away and top board in place.

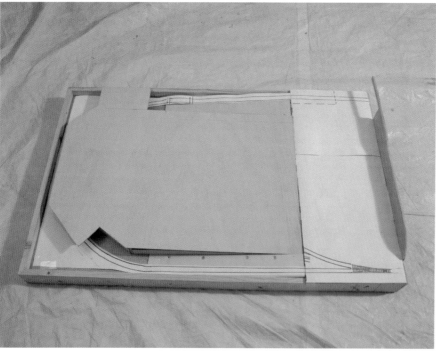

Top board fixed but with cut-away removed.

As with the level board, the transfer of the paper layout to the track is achieved by cutting the paper with a scalpel knife along the track lines and then inking in the score marks on the plywood. The whole board, like the flat board, only needs sanding down and painting.

The cut-away.

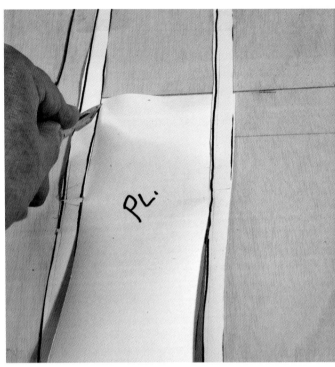

Transferring the plan to the board using a scalpel.

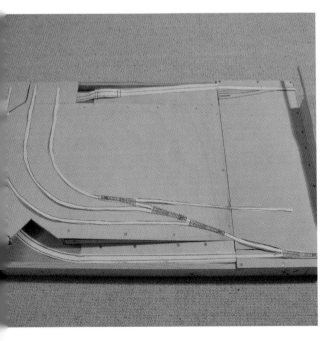

The cut out track showing only a small area of track is located on the cut out. This will be at the end of a station platform.

Transferring the track cuts to the board with a felt pen.

THE DROP BASEBOARD

If we look at how railways were first constructed you appreciate that the land with all its lumps, bumps and depressions existed and the railway company had to create as level a track as possible across this terrain. Whilst the norm for many layouts is a totally flat base, larger layouts and many club layouts try to emulate real life. The hidden marshalling yards are usually kept at one level as they have no scenery and this area is purely functional, but as you come round from this level you can install a drop baseboard and then support the track off the ground, allowing the scenery to ebb and flow both below and above the level of the track. The other alternative, as I have described here, is to have a specific feature, such as a valley, which requires a dropped section. Due to space limitations I have just inserted a narrow (500mm/19¾in) dropped section, but there is no reason why that dropped area could not have been much bigger or even the full width of the visible area. The principles are the same. The drop should never start on the joint between two boards.

As far as I am personally concerned the drop baseboard has a twofold purpose. First, it provides an opportunity, if required, to extend my existing baseboards from 3,300mm (130in) to 3,800mm (149½in). Second, I have created a deep trough that will become a feature, with a steep-sided valley and a canal stretching from .back to front of valley with a canal lock which will hopefully simulate rise and fall of water in a canal lock.

As far as this book is concerned it demonstrates how to create a valley in a full-sized or smaller board. The makeup of the frame is the same as other boards and like the multi-level board, it uses a frame of 69mm (27¼in). It is the same depth from back to front 700mm (27¼in) but only 500mm (20in) wide, as opposed to the 1,100mm (43in) main boards. I have made it this size as my railway room is only 4,000mm (157½in) long. I can fit three boards each of 1,100mm (43in) long plus a 500mm (19¾in) board along one wall and it can all be transported to exhibitions when required.

To bring the track across between the two adjoining boards there will be a small level area on each side before the valley. The tracks will traverse this

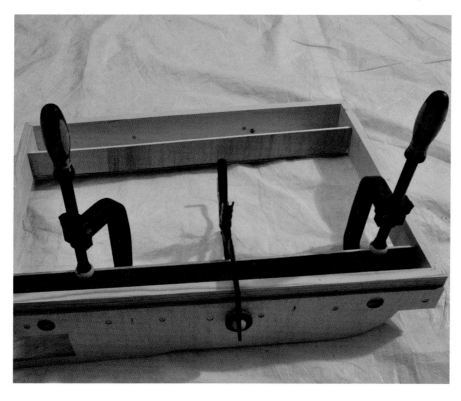

The drop baseboard frame being held in place until the glue dries.

The completed 500mm (19½in) board with both a level run-on and a level run-off with the centre drop, which will become a valley, with a bridge carrying the track at the back and an embankment at the front.

valley, with an embankment at the front and a bridge at the back. The level areas at each end are 100mm (4in) at one end and 60mm (2½in) wide at the other, leaving a valley of 340mm (13½in). Having had these pieces cut to the correct size, I have screwed and glued both to the frame. To support the level areas I have added 57mm (2¼in) deep cross-members (the cross-member will fit under the 6mm/¼in base-board top and have the 6mm (¼in) lower baseboard attached at the other end, making 69mm (2¾in) in total). These cross-members are located at the ends of the two short baseboards, as this is where the valley will begin. These form the vertical walls of the valley. These were glued and then clamped in position and left to dry overnight. The base of the trough is constructed from a sheet of 6mm (¼in) plywood, bringing the overall depth to 69mm (2¾in) – the same as the frame. This is glued to the two cross-

members and the two frame edges exactly in line with the base of the frame. This creates a vertical sided wooden 'well', which will be infilled with sloping sides and the canal at the modelling stage.

This completes the basic structure of the drop baseboard. Like all the other baseboards described in this book, it obviously needs sanding down and varnishing to produce the finished baseboard ready for modelling.

OPEN BASEBOARDS

Open-topped baseboards tend to be used where there are varying track levels and where there is only a minimal amount of track. Once again it is essential that you have a detailed track plan, so that you can work out the different heights of the track supports and the pattern required for the cross-members, before you begin. The plan must be to cut each cross-member from a single piece of plywood and in doing so to allow for both the planned design of the track(s) and the various heights. Obviously there is a slight loss in rigidity, as there is no overall baseboard top to hold the construction firmly. I would always recommend using a softwood frame. This is constructed in the same way as described for the flat-topped baseboard. When gluing it together, greater care has to be taken to ensure that all the corners are at 90 degrees, as you do not have a rectangular top to ensure accuracy. The final gluing can still be achieved by clamping each corner to a flat sheet of professionally cut wood. When dry, I prefer to add a small block of wood into each corner. I suggest that the minimum size should be 44mm (1¾in) by 44mm (1¾in) for the full depth of the frame.

The next stage is to add the cross-members in the same way as described earlier. The big difference is that the cross-members need to be cut to the correct height to support different track levels by using either a fret saw or a jig saw to cut the cross-member to predetermined heights. You will need slightly more cross-members to support the track than you would with a flat baseboard. Each cross-member must stretch the full width of the frame and they must be fitted vertically to provide maximum rigidity. Once in position and thoroughly dry, you need to insert the spine between the cross-members and the frame. Depending on the width of the board, you may need two spines.

You should now have a rigid frame with its spine and cross-members ready for the next stage. With an open board you are not installing a baseboard top, but you are fixing track beds for all the tracks. It is usually necessary to use a jig saw or a fretsaw, as tracks are unlikely to be straight lines. Each of the track beds is glued and either pin-nailed or screwed to each cross-member. Once all the track beds are in place, the skeleton of the frame will still be visible in many areas. These gaps are covered over with scenery or buildings made as part of the landscaping of the board. Once all the woodwork is complete, the board will require sanding and finishing.

The open baseboard with the contours cut into the cross-members and the only areas supported are the track beds where the three tracks will run.

INSULATION BOARD AS A BASEBOARD

Insulation board such as 'Celotex' can be used in certain situations. Some modellers push material uses to the extreme, but in this book I am limiting uses to the practical side. Insulation board is extremely light – a sheet of 50mm (2in) x 2,440 (96in) x 1,220 (48in) board can be picked up with two fingers. It has the disadvantage that it can be easily damaged. It is not cheap to buy, being slightly dearer that the equivalent size in 6mm (¼in) plywood. It was first used in the USA, where layouts tend to be much bigger and have longer track runs without points and signals. For those exhibiting their layouts with long runs and few points, such boards have a tremendous weight advantage. Track can be easily pinned or glued and pinned, but fixing point motors means either cutting a chunk out of the polystyrene-type foam and fixing the point directly to the track, or having surface point-motors.

The sides and ends of insulation boards need protection and if you have more than one board, they need to be joined together accurately. These boards, therefore, need a wooden frame to be constructed to your chosen size. This frame is constructed in the same way as with the standard baseboard fame. Cutting Celotex insulation board (or any other make) is easy. It can be achieved with a standard hand saw or a tenon saw, or even a serrated bread knife. The Celotex should be cut very slightly oversize (about 2mm) and glue applied to the sides of the frame – the glue must be 'Gripfix' or something similar, which does not dissolve the foam. The foam can then be squeezed into the frame, as it has a very small amount of flexibility. Use a length of flat wood rested on the Celotex and push (or use a mallet) to force home the Celotex. If you do not use something that spreads the load, you could crack the sheet. It is then possible to fit pattern makers' dowels into the wooden frame and, although you cannot fit bolts to join the boards, you can fit toggle catches to the frame (see Chapter 10). As there is no strength in the insulation board it is usual to support such boards on trestles, with supports running between them, or tables. Unless weight reduction is crucial, or unless you just wish to experiment, I would personally not recommend the use of insulation boards. The weight saving between a 6mm (¼in) top with 6mm (¼in) cross-members and the weight of Celotex is not that great as to make any crucial difference.

Insulation board 50mm (2in) and its frame.

Using a tenon saw to cut insulation board – note the lack of bits compared with cutting polystyrene.

ABOVE: *The pre-glued frame with insulation board squeezed into it. Note that the frame is glued around the top of the upright so that as the Celotex is pushed home, it spreads downwards. If the Celotex had been glued, all the glue would have remained on the surface due to the tight fit.*

LEFT: *The completed board.*

COOPERATIVE CONSTRUCTION

In several clubs and national organizations, there are some groups who wish to work cooperatively to produce personally designed individual boards that join together to make a much larger layout. The key to such projects is a master set of end patterns that allow individuals to produce their own board, knowing that, having used the standard end pattern to fit the joining dowels, both the tracks and the baseboards will line up exactly with any other baseboard in the same scheme. Probably the most well-known is 'FREMO,' a large international group of railway modellers who organise meetings all over Europe. The individual personal layouts all have the same end plates and, therefore, will join together in any combination at an exhibition. Their longest layout is reported to be 1.2km. Further information on the organization is available on www.fremo-net.eu.

Most clubs, when building a multi-board layout, will use a standard end pattern so that all boards are the same and could be put together in a variety of ways. The 'OO' section of my own club has planned a new exhibition layout, but as a result of moving to new premises, has decided to use the fiddle yards at each end only for exhibitions and replace them with alternative boards to create a continuous circuit for club use. Likewise the 'N'-gauge section of the club is also building a new layout, which can be expanded for display at exhibitions by the addition of two 1000mm (39in) boards both in the back and the front of the layout. (Unlike the 'OO'-gauge section this will be continuous running for exhibitions and within the club – it will just be longer at exhibitions!) These developments will not be possible without standard end plates. Whilst we can design our own unique end panels, many members are also members of the local 'N' Society group who are also planning cooperative

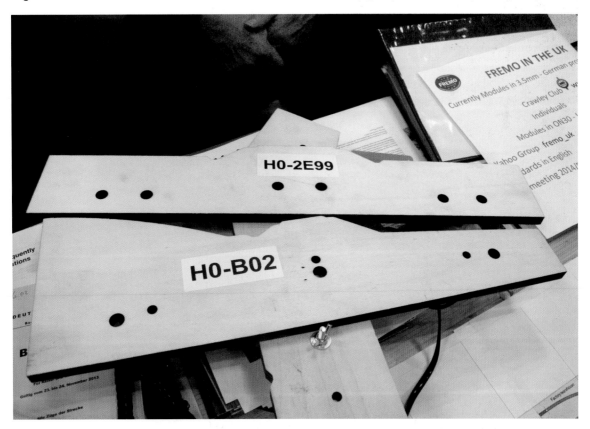

A sample set of 'FREMO' end jigs.

A homemade wooden jig with its end stop. The central board allows the jig to fit both left- and right-hand end boards.

The jig placed over the end of a baseboard.

The pilot hole at the front of the jig. (There is a second hole towards the rear.)

board construction. Both groups have investigated having a pattern made in metal, so that all members can drill their own boards to exactly accurate pre-determined holes, but the normal costs of a metal pattern are high and there is a general feeling that if a national manufacturer was prepared to market a reasonably priced standard end panel for a variety of widths, e.g. 450mm (17¾in), 600mm (23½in) and 700mm (28in) wide, there would be a considerable market across many societies and clubs, and possibly the creation of a national standard. In the meantime, an alternative is to use a wooden pattern. The pattern has to fit on the edge of a board so that its pre-drilled hole or holes are both at the same height from the top of the board and the same distance from the ends. A simple 'T' constructed in 18mm (¾in) by 69mm (2¾in) softwood (or hardwood), with an end stop and a single hole, will provide such a pattern. The only use of the pattern is to accurately position the centre of the dowel holes (and bolt holes if used). The actual drilling of the holes to accommodate the plate of the dowel is all based on the pilot holes. The

design of this pattern means that it can be turned round to allow use on both corners and, no matter which way round the board is used, the dowel holes will marry up exactly. By fitting a male dowel to the front of the end panel and a female dowel to the rear of the end panel, boards can be interlinked.

THE ACCESS FLAP

Layouts in lofts, specific railway rooms or 'dens' will often be end-to-end layouts. Many modellers prefer layouts that have continuous running. Taking a layout in a shed, for example, it is possible to have a track running from one side of the door to the other, with each end being much wider to allow the track to curve back on itself. In this way you get continuous running and free access into the centre of the layout. The alternative is to have a hinged or removable flap to permit access. It may also be that the layout is sufficiently high so that the owner and visitors are able to duck under the layout, but this is less popular as you get older.

The additional end plate attached to the baseboard. The ends are chamfered to prevent catching clothes on a sharp corner.

Hinged flaps obviously rely on a hinge. There are specialist bar hinges, which have to be cut into the worktop, but they still have some flexibility in the opposite end and need to have a method of ensuring that the track is 100 per cent lined up each time. Hinged flaps are very heavily used and over a period of time can become a little slack. The best system is a drop-in section. The frame of the section needs to be very rigid and it is probably best to use 44mm (1¾in) square timber for the frame, covered in 6m (1/8in) plywood to create the baseboard.

The two main baseboard ends need to have lips added to support the drop-in section. These need to be 34mm (1¼in) by 44mm (1¾in) to provide sufficient strength and rigidity. The lips need to be glued and screwed to the layout ends at a level that is 50mm (2in) below the baseboard surface (to accommodate the depth of the drop in frame and its baseboard).

The width of 44mm (1¾in) is essential. To ensure complete registry between tracks on the drop-in section and the main baseboard ends you need to fit furniture-makers' dowels. These are not fitted to the sides, but to the bottom of the drop-in section and the top of the lips. As they need to be an exact register, it is best to either drill both the shelf and the drop frame before they are fixed, or use a standard jig. As the tracks are laid after fitting, you only need to be concerned with the height of the drop-in section in relation to the main baseboards and lining up the edges of both with the drop-in section. Once complete, the drop-in section can be easily lifted out and dropped back in with certainty that the tracks will line up. To provide even more stability it is sensible to use toggle clamps so that the section cannot inadvertently be removed.

ABOVE: *Dowels are inserted in the top of the end plate and the bottom of the flap. Be careful to position the two frames correctly before drilling. One will be upside down.*

RIGHT: *The new flap fitted on to the chamfered end plate to create a level join.*

NOVELTY BASEBOARDS

There has been a tendency in the last few years for a series of novelty baseboards to be produced, usually with a very simple oval with one siding. An old computer monitor case has been used containing a Wild West scene. A bigger layout is contained in a car roof top box, which opened up to provide lighting and a reasonably complex layout. This can be closed up easily and fitted back on the roof of the car for transporting back home. A multitude of small aluminium or other rigid material suitcases also appear at some shows, with a variety of layouts and scenery. Each layout and baseboard has to be designed for each situation. All three examples have flat baseboards supported to a suitable height for viewing.

There are many variations of novelty baseboards which are seen at shows. Some have been produced for specific competitions, but others have been purely for a weekend project. It can make a change for a serious modeller to have fun occasionally and it certainly causes comment from the exhibition viewing public.

FINISHING THE BASEBOARD

Having reached almost the end of the chapter, you will have constructed your baseboard in whatever design you have chosen. The first task, before proceeding further, is to check that all the joints and seams are well-glued, adding a little extra glue where it has not fully taken. You will need to double check that all the screws are tight and that all the pin nails are tapped fully home, using a centre punch.

At some stage you will probably be adding a mixture of water and PVA to various parts of your layout on the baseboard. Much will depend on the type of layout being planned for the board. You need to both sand and seal the board to stop the ingress of any water into any of the joints (remember most PVA glues are still water soluble)

Further information on finishing is contained in Chapter 9.

FINAL COMMENTS

By now you have all the information you need to construct a wide range of baseboards. The choice is obviously yours, depending on your skills and the availability of tools. It is important that you use the instructions given regarding the flat baseboard as the basic for the construction of many other types of board, as the basic information is not repeated for each board. I have assumed that you have read the book thoroughly before starting to work on your board.

WHAT IF I DO NOT HAVE THE WOODWORKING SKILLS?

If you take your time and follow the instructions, creating a simple baseboard is not beyond the scope of most railway modellers. If you feel it is beyond your capabilities, you may find someone at your local club who can assist.

In Chapter 15 you will find instructions on building a very simple baseboard with legs that requires only glue and a screwdriver and a local DIY centre to do all your cutting. Personally, it is not a board I would recommend unless you are really stuck, as it is a little 'clunky' and heavy, but it will do the job if you do not have the skill or the courage to build a more complicated board or the funds to buy a commercial one. If I did not have the skills I would prefer the board described in Chapter 16 to a second-hand one off the internet.

If all else fails, there are manufacturers of model railway baseboards who sell either completed boards or boards in kit form, which require the minimum of skill to produce a satisfactory baseboard. Chapter 14 gives more details and Chapter 16 concentrates on constructing the simplest baseboard of all, for which you only need a screwdriver and some glue.

CHAPTER EIGHT

THE FOLDING BASEBOARD

I have separated this baseboard into its own chapter because, although it follows many of the basics in flat-baseboard construction, it has many variations and several different methods of achieving the construction. This especially relates to the background and the joining of the two boards. The main aim of this board was to produce a simpler board to allow easy transportation and erection, and I plan to use it when putting on a small display in a village hall, or for a local charity, or where set-up time is very limited. It could equally be used at home where you need a good layout that will store easily and in a relatively small space (cupboard, wardrobe or similar). This board also supports a lighting stand, which is described in Chapter 12. This chapter deals in detail with the construction of such a board.

BOARD CONSTRUCTION

JOINING BOARDS

Most multiple board layouts are joined end-to-end, but it can be beneficial to join baseboards along their length. One advantage is that you can still have a complicated layout on display without too many joins crossing between the two boards. A second advantage is that the width of the board can be 50 per cent narrower than the traditional continuous-run board. This has advantages when transporting layouts to shows and manoeuvring through doors and corridors to reach a specific show location. Storage between shows is made simpler, as such a layout will often fit in a tall cupboard.

I have described the whole process, as there several differences in the sequence that things need to be achieved. For example, the backboard is one of the final attachments to a normal board, but the inclusion of the backboard comes at a very early stage, as it has to be fitted between the two halves of the board.

FRAMES

First, the frames have to be cut to the correct length and width, in this case 1,500mm (59in) by 450mm (17¾in). I always mitre corners, as I feel it gives a greater bond and ensures better right-angles. There is no reason why the corners cannot be butt jointed, but both the back and the front frame sections must be exactly the same length to allow the fitting of the toggle clamps. I have made both the back and the front the same depth, but the back can be much narrower if you do not want multiple storage tracks out of sight. Making them both the same, makes it easier to close the two units for transporting.

As with all other baseboards you need to make up the frame first. This allows you to take accurate measurements of the actual frame, rather than relying on paper measurements. The more accurate you are, the more accurate will be the fit of the baseboard top and the cross-members.

BASEBOARD TOPS

As described earlier in the book, it is best to have the tops of the baseboards cut professionally and for this you need a cutting list and plan. You need to work out the various lengths and widths of timber you require and create a list, keeping like sizes together. From this list you need to draw up the various sized boards you require on to a scale drawing of a standard sheet of 6mm (¼in) (or other thickness) board. By careful positioning you will be able to keep wastage to a minimum and make cutting as easy as possible. If you just provide a cutting list, the sheet timber will be cut in the most convenient way for the person doing the

The two identical frames making up the two halves of the board.

cutting, which may not be the most economical way of utilizing the standard timber sheet.

Having the sheet timber cut professionally will ensure that the boards accurately fit the measurements you have taken from the frame you have constructed, and that the sides and ends are at true right-angles.

BACKGROUND

It is at this early stage that the background must be considered and allowed for, as you need to include the background board and end boards in your calculations and cutting list.

Once cut, push the two halves of the baseboard together, with the background board sandwiched vertically between them.

Next, loosely place the baseboard top of the front section close to the upright background and draw a line on the background board delineating the position of the baseboard top. Following your previously drawn out track plan, mark the background where the tracks pass through the background. Use a tunnel entrance as a 'former', to mark out the correct position of the tunnel at each end. Mark both the shape of the tunnel and the width. Remove the tunnel 'former' and draw lines slightly narrower than the outer width of the tunnel 'former' and also slightly lower than the top, but slightly wider than the actual opening.

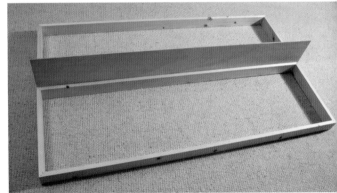

The background board sandwiched between the two frames.

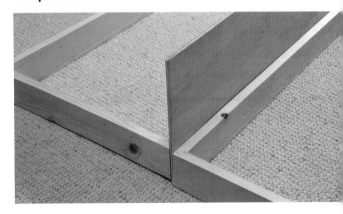

Close-up of the background board and two frames. Note the background is exactly the same length as the frame.

Having laid the baseboard top on to the front frame, draw a line at baseboard height.

Mark the centre of the proposed tunnel at each end of the background.

Use an old tunnel entrance as a guide.

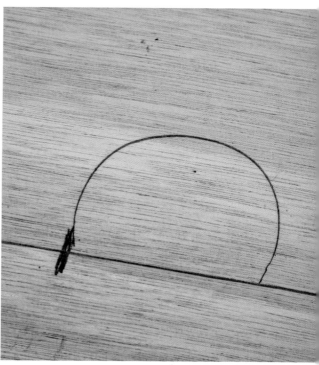

Draw the outline of the tunnel.

You also need to remove an area half-way between the two tunnel entrances, but this must be kept shorter than the height of the frame of the baseboard. Remove the background board from between the two frames and use a jig saw or fret saw to cut out the three marked panels. The centre panel will have been cut to the correct height but the two tunnel entrances will require a further cut. Using the previously marked horizontal line of the baseboard top, cut the entrances in half and discard the top half.

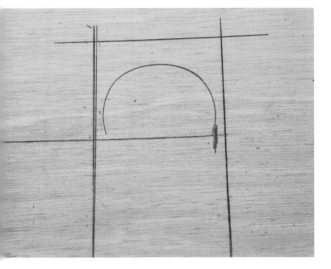

Also mark the outer limits of the tunnel wall.

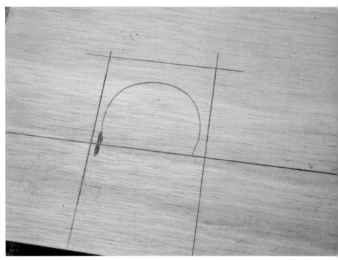

This needs to be marked out for each of the two tunnels, as you will have to cut wider than the actual tunnel but not as wide as the outer limits of the tunnel wall. You also need to carry the outer lines to the bottom of the background board as a cutting guide.

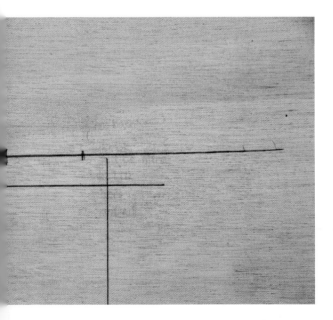

The centre cut-out must again go to the bottom of the background board but must fall short of the baseboard level. This cut-out is purely to support the central dowel in line with the two outside ones.

Using a fret saw (it is just as simple to use a fine-bladed jig saw) to cut just inside the line of the outer wall limit.

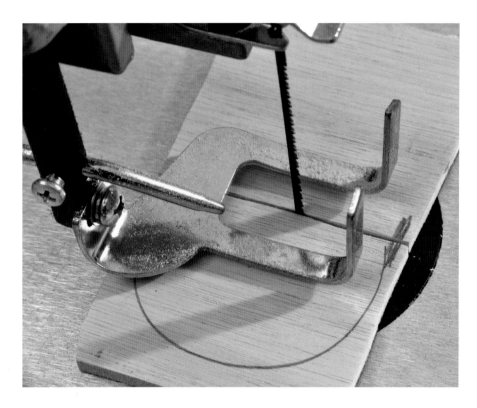

Having completely cut out the two tunnel entrances, you need to cut across the removed piece at baseboard level.

Care needs to be taken with the next stage. Clamp the background board with its three cut-outs to the front frame. Next, slide the centre cut-out into the gap, and do the same with the remaining pieces of the tunnel entrances. (Make sure you get them the correct way round.) When you are sure that all three fit perfectly, glue and clamp each one into place, ensuring that no glue gets on to the main background board.

The bottom piece is replaced into the background to leave the open tunnel, with the background board base being inserted. It must be at baseboard top level, not level with the top of the frame. This provides a level bed for the track.

The background board in place ready for the centre piece to be fitted into the gap below baseboard level.

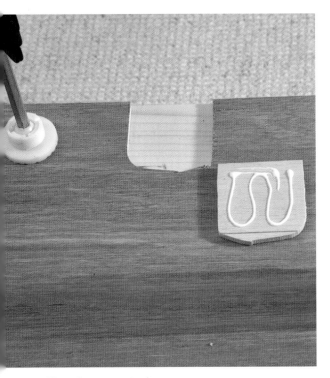

Glue the cut out piece.

Clamp it into the gap until the glue is dry.

As soon as all three cut-outs are in place, remove the background board, just leaving the three pieces in place.

The background hole for the tunnels will reach from the bottom of the baseboard to the top of the tunnel, with only the tunnel mouth being open.

Glue the bottom piece of the tunnel.

Level it with the bottom of the frame and clamp it with the top protruding the frame.

Clamping it in this position will leave it level with the baseboard top when fitted.

View from inside the frame showing it above frame height.

All three cut-outs should be level with the base of the frame. The centre cut-out top should be lower than the top of the baseboard level, but the tunnel entrances must be level with the baseboard top when it is fitted, so they will stand proud at the moment. Leave these to dry overnight.

Having glued the two frames you need to mark the positioning holes for the dowels between the two frames to ensure correct alignment. You need to do this before the baseboard tops and cross-members are fitted to permit accurate drilling. If the top or a cross-member has been fitted it is unlikely that you will be able to get the drill at an exact right angle to the side of the frame. You have to drill from the inside in order to go through both frames together and at a right angle.

As the boards are being joined lengthways, I am inserting a third dowel to ensure 100 per cent accuracy. The third dowel will be located centrally, whilst the other dowels will be placed centrally to the track joins at either end, to ensure maximum accuracy. I am, therefore, not using a standard jig, but ensuring accuracy by clamping the two frames together.

DOWELS

The next task is to remove the main background board and, ensuring that the tops of the two frames are exactly level and are fully level from side to side, clamp them firmly together and drill a pilot hole, using a 2.5mm (^{1}/$_{20}$in) drill bit, through both frames in the centre of each of the blocks you have glued to the front board. To ensure accuracy, insert wooden spacers to stop the clamped frame from flexing, as you will have to clamp on either side of the blocks to allow space for the pilot hole to be drilled. Once this is complete, separate the two frames and glue and screw the tops to the two baseboards, ensuring that they are flush on all sides.

The best way is to line up the baseboard top with both ends and one side, and fix this with screws at each corner and in the centre. You can then slightly adjust the frame to bring it into square with the baseboard. When you have made these small adjustments, you will be able to line the ends up with the ends of the top and then you can screw both tops all the way round. Leave these until fully dry.

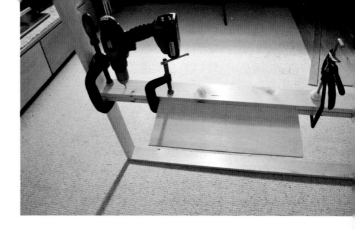

When the glue is dry, either replace the background or add small sheets of wood, so that the two frames can be clamped together. You need to keep the three cut-outs free of clamps to allow you to drill through them.

Drill pilot holes through both frames and the centre of each cut-out.

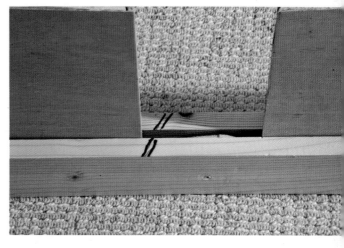

Note the markings on one tunnel entrance between the two baseboards, so that they will be drilled for the dowels correctly.

CLOCKWISE, FROM TOP LEFT:

Having had the top cut professionally, drill and countersink a series of holes around the perimeter.

Make sure you have a screwdriver and sufficient screws.

Glue the frame.

Once the tops are fully dry, you can drill the holes required to fit the jointing dowels. You need to work from the outside of the frame and use a 25mm (1in) spade drill. Using the marker hole that you made from the inside of the frame, insert the point of your spade drill and slowly and carefully drill a hole just deep enough to sink the base of the dowel, so that the top is almost flush with the side of the baseboard. Do this on both baseboards, but on the baseboard to be fitted with the female dowels, drill a 10mm ($^3/_{10}$in) hole, again using the pilot hole as the centre, to permit the male end of the dowel to sink into the brass dowel and the frame. Take a smaller 16mm ($^1/_2$in) spade drill and remove a minute layer of wood. (Spade drills are not totally flat and using a smaller drill removes the very tiny lump of wood surrounding the pilot hole.) Screw

CLOCKWISE, FROM TOP LEFT:

Line it up with one side and the two corners.

Insert three screws along one side – one in each corner and one in the centre.

If the frame is slightly out of true (this has been exaggerated for photographic clarity), push the frame into square with the baseboard, scew up all the screws and leave overnight to dry.

the female dowel firmly in position with three screws and fix the male dowel with one well-tightened screw. Push the two units together and ensure that they are entirely level. Once you are happy, pull the two carefully apart and insert a further screw in each of the male dowels and tighten. Check alignment once again and, if still correct, insert and tighten the third screw. If it is not correct, remove the second screw, retighten the first screw and push together again. Ease apart again and insert a screw into the third hole. Tighten and recheck the fitting until the two boards line up correctly, then insert the final screw and retighten. If you need to make more attempts to get the two boards level, take out all the screws from the male dowel and twist the dowel so that you have new wood into which you can screw.

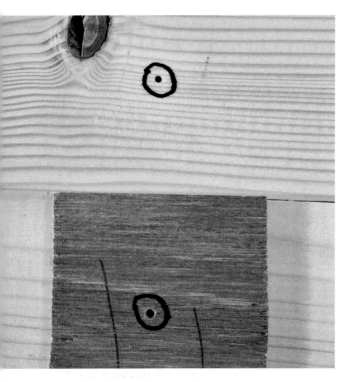

Locate the pilot holes for the dowels.

Use a 25mm (1in) spade drill.

Cut out for the dowel to the correct depth to allow the dowel plate to be just above the surface of the frame.

Use a 16mm ($^5/_8$in) spade drill to take out the centre bump, leaving a level clean hole for the dowel.

The dowel will now sit comfortably in the hole.

A hole needs to be bored behind the cut for the female dowel. Use a male dowel to ensure it will fully sink into the hole.

Screw in a couple of screws tightly into the female dowel.

Insert one screw tightly into the male dowel.

Next you need to clamp the two baseboards together. Ensure that they are on a level surface and that you engage the dowels. Check that the tops of the boards are exactly level, especially at the tunnel entrances.

Interlock the two dowels and check that the two baseboards are level.

Refit the removable background board to check that everything fits.

END PANELS

The next stage is to fit the background boards. You will have already cut and tested the background board but, to help with the stability of the whole unit when transported, I suggest permanently fixing the two end panels to the front baseboard. These need to be fixed flush with the bottom of the base at the two ends of the front board, glued and clamped. As the background board is 240mm (9½in) high, the two end panels also need to be the same height above baseboard level. Using clamps, lock the two boards together.

Glue the end panel of the front baseboard and clamp it into place.

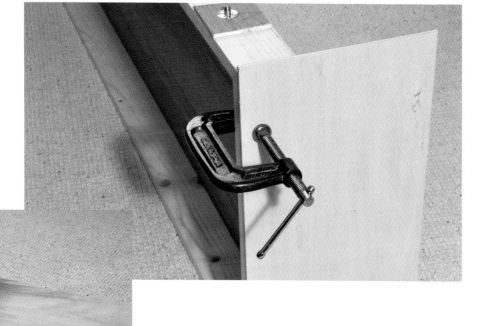

The end panel for the front baseboard in place.

Check that the end panel and the background panel meet in the corners.

Each end of the rear baseboard needs to have a plywood panel from back to front and from the base of the panel up to about 10mm ($^3/_{10}$in) from the top of the board. On the outside of this you need to add a further panel with the same dimensions, except that it should stand 30mm (1¼in) above the level of the baseboard top. This will create a small groove into which the two front board end panels will slot, when the back baseboard is turned upside down on top of the front baseboard.

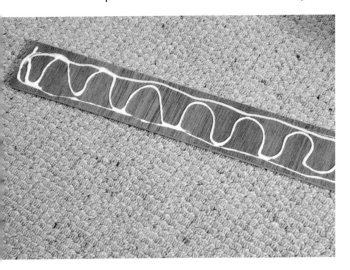

Glue a small extra strip of plywood.

Clamp it to the side of the rear baseboard and repeat at the other end. This strip must be below the level of the baseboard top.

Cut and glue a further piece of plywood, which will stand slightly above the level of the baseboard. This creates a groove at each end between the top of the baseboard and the side panel.

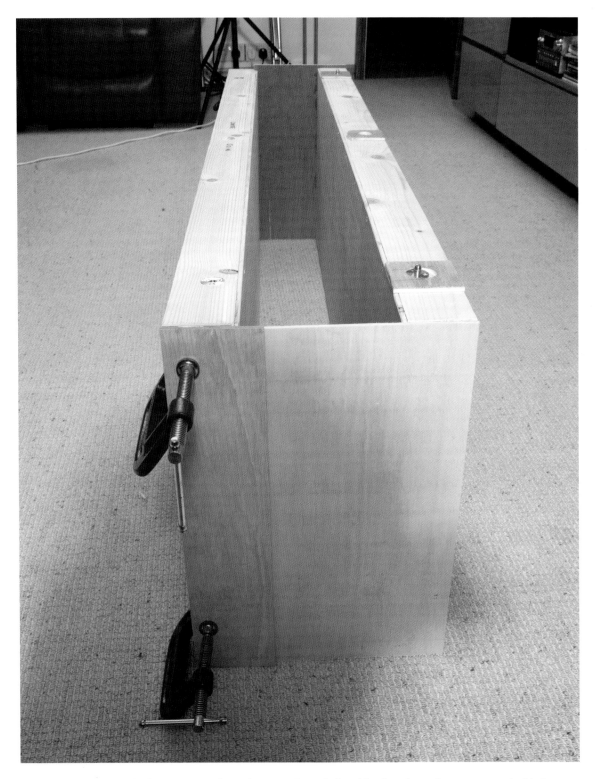

When closed up ready for transporting, the top edge of the side slots into the groove to hold the two halves together.

The two units when joined in this way create the two sides of the box to be transported. When the layout is completed, all the track, etc., is contained within the box and is protected. The picture shows it being tested before the final end panel is glued into place.

JOINTING CLAMPS

You are now in a position to fit jointing clamps. I have found that it is best to use 'Adjustable Toolbox Toggle Clamps'. The adjustable ones are slightly more expensive than the fixed ones but both allow for long-term wear and, more importantly, for ease of fitting. Screw in the adjustable side, ensuring that it will easily link to the hook side and that neither overlaps the divide between the two boards. Adjust the toggle from the position supplied by the manufacturer by turning the screw. Moving the threaded toggle further on to the thread before you fix the clamp will allow greater adjustment, as the man-

ufacturers give the minimum number of turns to hold the item together. Close the toggle as though it was fastened and then screw to the baseboard side. When fixed and without undoing the catch, slide the hook side into position and screw into place. Pull the handle to release the clamp and tighten the thread a couple of turns and re-clamp the two together. If it is too tight, slacken off the thread, or if it is still too slack, tighten the thread. The ideal should be a clamp that requires a little resistance when locking into place.

The completed baseboard now requires lighting to be added (*see* Chapter 12).

The fitted toggle clamp.

The completed board with its lighting stand and track plan.

CLOSING THE BASEBOARDS FOR STORAGE AND TRANSPORTATION

The two end panels will have some form of scenery on the inside, but, apart from a very small piece at the top where they fit into the groove, there is unlikely to be any damage as the insides do not rub against anything when closing.

The first task is to dismantle the lighting stand and fit the top panel inside the front panel.

Next, fasten the two uprights to the top of the rear baseboard using bolts and wing nuts.

Slide the top lighting panel inside the front lighting panel.

Fasten the uprights to the rear baseboard.

Use wing nuts rather than ordinary nuts.

Fold the back baseboard upside down on top of the front baseboard, ensuring that the sides fit into the grooves.

Take the two handles and screw them into place between the front and back boards.

With the handles firmly fixed, turn the unit over and lay the two lighting boards along the other side and bolt into position.

Ensure the two baseboards fit together with the front baseboard sides fitting into the groove created on the rear baseboard.

Fit the handles. Note that there is an extra block of plywood at one end. This is to ensure the handles fit level as the background board is not as wide as the lighting boards.

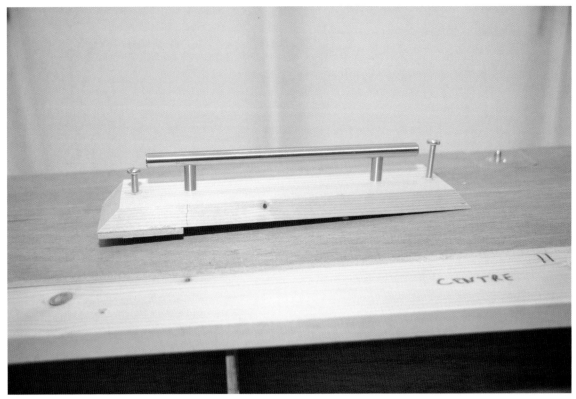

The extra wood fits over the lip of the backboard and holds it in place.

Fit both handles and use bolts and wing nuts.

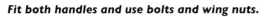

Fit the two boards of the lighting unit to the opposite side of the 'folded' baseboards to the handles.

The lighting uprights are stowed comfortably inside the unit.

The two lighting uprights, having been fixed to the rear baseboard, are contained within the completed box.

The total layout is contained as one unit, with only the rolling stock and power supply being separate.

When all bolted together, it creates an elongated 'brief case' some 1,520mm (60in) x 605mm (24in) x 305mm (12in) with carrying handles. The layout is sufficiently protected both for transit in a car or between car and exhibition venue.

It is light enough to carry with the two handles, or it can be wheeled on a trolley. For protection I usually use two rubber 'spider' clips. It was designed to fit in my car with just the single rear passenger seat either folded down or removed.

The completed unit is easily carried.

Having completed the construction you now have the enjoyable task of fitting the track, the electrics and the scenery and, of course, running the trains.

It can also be transported on a folding trolley.

When using a trolley it is best to attach rubber 'spiders' to stop any slippage.

With the single seat folded down or removed, the whole unit takes up little space in the car.

CHAPTER NINE

SANDING AND FINISHING

GENERAL COMMENT

No matter how accurate your construction work and how well your layout is prepared, the style and quality of the final product will be the one thing that projects your image in the minds of the viewers of your layout. It is, therefore, essential that you spend time on the final processes of your baseboard construction. All too often there is a desire to push on to get the track laid and to have an operating layout, but you should only start this task when all the filling, sanding and painting are complete.

FILLING

There will be a multitude of countersunk screw holes on the baseboard top. All of these need filling with a quality wood-filler, which needs to be worked into each screw hole. Using cheap filler will result in it falling out at some time in the future, so it is best

Filler and plastic filler spatula.

Use a wide spatula to fill in screw holes on a baseboard top.

to buy a good one rather than a cheap one. After all you will not need a great deal of filler to cover every indentation.

SANDING

Every part of the wooden structure should be sanded down with fine-grade sandpaper. This can either be achieved with a power sander or by hand with sheet sandpaper and a cork (or other) block. All parts, from the bottom of the leg to the top of the backboard, should be finished as smooth as possible before proceeding further.

When completed, all the dust should be removed. A powerful vacuum with a brush attachment is one way. The brush is most important as it will drag out any loose dust that just a vacuum leaves behind. A more effective way, if you have one, is to use a garden leaf-blower, without its collection bag. Obviously this needs to be done outside, as otherwise you will spread the dust everywhere.

A detail sander is used to level the surface when hard dry.

Painting the baseboard top will, with some paints, obliterate the track plan.

VARNISHING AND PAINTING

The whole board needs to be either painted or varnished. The baseboard top needs to be coated in an earth colour, so that any chips or loss of scatter from the baseboard does not reveal a white patch. As you are probably laying scatter and track, you will be wetting the baseboard with varying quantities of water, so you need to seal the wood before any water is able to soak in and damage the surface. If you paint the baseboard top in a dark matt colour, you may, of course, obliterate the track markings that you previously marked out in pencil. If you used a sharp knife to mark the track position, these cuts should still be visible through the paint. You should still have the cut-out track plan, so it is not a difficult task to remark the position of each of the tracks if they do become obliterated.

The edges of the board need to be finished in a gloss in order to make the whole board more visually attractive and to protect the wood from grease through constant handling. I always prefer to use black gloss, but a regional railway colour is also appropriate. Use masking tape to create the straight edge when painting two different colours.

A completely covered board.

The underside of the board also needs painting. I prefer to use white or at least a very light colour – it makes the wiring stand out more clearly.

All of this will take time and cannot be rushed. You can only paint one side of your board at a time

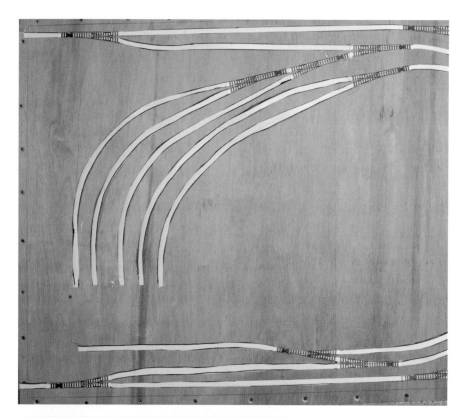

A track plan can be reused if the cut marks on the baseboard have been lost.

Masking tape provides a straight edge when joining different colours.

The white underside of a board. A white or light-coloured underside makes any subsequent wiring stand out and circuit information can be written directly on to the baseboard, rather than on a tag on the wire, which will come off or get ripped.

and you will need to allow plenty of drying time, especially for leg sockets and other removable parts. You need to allow about seven days for everything to be hard dry.

LEG ADJUSTERS

Whilst all your legs will be the same length, there will be occasions where you need some adjustment and it is best to fit height adjusters at the beginning. The easiest type screw to the side of the leg and are adjusted by using a screw driver on the adjusting thread.

An alternative height adjuster, which has to be drilled and screwed into the centre of the foot of the leg.

CHAPTER TEN

MULTIPLE BOARDS

Apart from the very smallest of layouts, it is almost certain that you will be using more than one board. There is a temptation, if the layout is an almost permanent fixture, to make it out of one continuous board, or at least several boards permanently fixed to each other and perhaps to a wall. I always caution against this as it usually causes major problems when rooms are required for other purposes, or decoration is required. It is far easier to have a couple of smaller boards that can be stored or moved and then connected together again.

DOWELS

There are always fears that the joins will not line up properly and that they will be a constant source of problems and derailments. If the work is done carefully and properly in the first place, joins will not create any greater risk of problems than any other part of the track. In the previous chapter I explained how to install male and female pattern-makers' dowels. These dowels will repeatedly align the two or more baseboards accurately. Pattern-makers' dowels are expensive, but worth every penny in terms of guaranteed accuracy. I would go

Male and female dowels.

as far as to say that they were essential in joining baseboards. You can buy cheaper brass dowels, but these are nowhere near as rigidly fixed as proper pattern-makers' dowels. Others will use wooden dowel pegs going into corresponding holes, but these have problems with wear over time. Using such cheaper versions leads to the myth that joining boards is difficult. Pattern-makers' dowels are accurate, with any slackness being measured in millionths of a centimetre.

BOLTS

As well as ensuring that boards meet together accurately, you need to lock them together. Some people just bolt baseboards together and rely on the bolt to provide an accurate register and a way of holding the board together. You can just make holes in the wood or, as described earlier, you can insert metal rods in the two frames. Using just bolts or bolts and rods means that when the bolts

are slid into position you have to manually line up the track each time, both vertically and horizontally. The variation will only be minute but it will be sufficient to derail a loco or carriages. Over time the wood will wear and the holes will very slowly enlarge, to make the alignment process even more difficult. Even using metal rods to preserve the accuracy of the hole, still leaves a little 'slack', which needs to be adjusted on each occasion.

Fixing boards together with bolts does require you to fiddle underneath both boards to attach wing nuts to the bolts. For older railway modellers this can be a little problematic and it is possible to catch some of the wires in the process, so it is probably not the best solution. Bolts have the advantage that everything is hidden and out of reach of tiny fingers at shows.

In running through the construction sequence, I have already explained how to join two or more boards together using bolts. The remainder of this chapter deals with other methods of joining boards.

Metal tube being inserted into a frame to prevent wear when inserting bolts.

Bolt and wing nut used to hold boards together.

HINGES

Hinges with loose pins are available from most DIY stores. To attach these, first ensure that the dowels are fully engaged, and then, using wood clamps, lock the two boards together. When you are happy that they are totally in line with each other, just screw the hinge vertically across the joint. When you want to separate the two boards, just tap out the centre pin. You will probably need a nail, narrower than the pin, to allow you to push the pin up and remove it. It is more practical to find a local metal worker and get him to add a 'T'-piece to the top of the pin to make it easier to pull out.

Hinges have the disadvantage that the remaining rings that hold the pin protrude beyond the edge of the board and must be allowed for when packing away. It also means that you cannot fasten anything totally flat to the front or back of the frame. I often fasten a sloping information board to the front of my layout when at exhibitions. Hinges have the advantage that you do not have to go under the board to make the connection. One of the big disadvantages is ensuring that the pin does not get lost when removed!

TOGGLE CATCHES

Toggle catches are, however, easier to fasten and to undo than hinges. It is better to pay a little more and get good quality toggle catches, as the hasp in some of the cheaper ones can stretch slightly, thus making the connection less solid. The best toggle catches are adjustable ones where the tension can be varied. This is by far the best method, with no parts to get lost, no fiddling underneath to join baseboards together and the ability to adjust the tension.

TAKING CARE

The tracks on multiple baseboards have, of necessity, to be absolutely in line and level with the ends of the boards. It is important that the last few sleepers are very well fixed and that ends are protected. The last part of each rail can be soldered to a screw inserted

Hinge with removable pin. The normal hinge pin has been removed and a bent rod has been inserted. This makes for easier removal when separating boards.

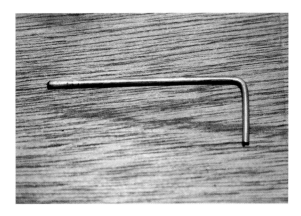

The pin – which is so easy to lose.

Adjusting a toggle clamp.

The closed toggle clamp holds the two boards together.

Door protector strip obtained from a builders' merchant.

Door protector strip on end of layout to protect rail ends.

into the frame of the baseboard, or you can solder the track to a 'paxolin' strip to strengthen the end. It is also possible to obtain shaped foam, which is often used as protection for high-quality doors and window frames. It is usually blue in colour and will stretch over the end of a board to protect each end in transit. A simple alternative is a length of wood and a simple clamp fitted over each end when the boards are being transported. The transport cases, which fit in my car, have a slot cut in them to protect the rail ends.

Cut-out in my transport box to protect rails. The baseboard rests against the inner layers of plywood and automatically locates the track within the recessed area.

CHAPTER ELEVEN

VIEWING HEIGHT AND SUPPORT SYSTEMS

VIEWING HEIGHT

There is no standard height for baseboards – it is purely a matter of personal choice. If your layout is purely for home use and mainly for young children, you will wish to have the baseboard at a suitable height for them, and as they grow you will probably wish to make the board higher. Hence it is better to have a free-standing baseboard, where the legs can be replaced or added to periodically.

There are many modellers who prefer people to view their layouts as though they are actually viewing on the ground, whilst others prefer to view layouts from slightly above, and still others who prefer to view the layout from about 45 degrees above.

For layouts used in a club there needs to be agreement across all the members, taking into account the differing heights of people and the fact that a good percentage of the time, members will be working on developing the layout. If you are working on a layout, it needs to be lower than if you are just running trains, because you need to be able to access each part with ease.

If the layout is to be displayed in an exhibition, there are a range of other considerations. It is normally accepted that layouts will be a little too high for children and many parents will bring a small stool or just lift children up. It is a good idea, as practiced at many exhibition venues, to have small stools available for the children whose parents are first-time visitors and who have no stool.

If I had to suggest a suitable height, I would say that the most popular height is just under 1,000mm (39in) high. To some younger people this will give an eye-level view, whilst others will see the layout from above, but it appears to be a reasonable compromise height. Some exhibitors go as high as 1,300mm (51in).

No matter what height you decide upon, the boards need to be stable and secure. There are a variety of ways to achieve this.

SUPPORT SYSTEMS

TABLES

The simplest support is to put the baseboard on a table. If this is to be the case, you have to ensure that all the wires for power, switches and so on, come through the side rather than underneath the baseboard. It is probably best to have stubby legs in each of the corners, fastened to a flat board across each pair, with each baseboard covered with felt or similar material to stop the table top being scratched, whilst lifting the board a couple of inches clear. Using the same softwood as the frame, cut two corner pieces

Corner cut and glued to frame leg.

Corner fitted and screwed into place.

Stubby leg being tested before chamfering.

End of leg glued ready for cross-plate.

With legs in place, screw in the cross-plate to both legs.

The chamfer the tops of the stubby legs so that they slide in with ease but tighten as pushed home.

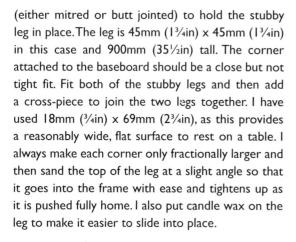

Legs with cross-plate.

(either mitred or butt jointed) to hold the stubby leg in place. The leg is 45mm (1¾in) x 45mm (1¾in) in this case and 900mm (35½in) tall. The corner attached to the baseboard should be a close but not tight fit. Fit both of the stubby legs and then add a cross-piece to join the two legs together. I have used 18mm (¾in) x 69mm (2¾in), as this provides a reasonably wide, flat surface to rest on a table. I always make each corner only fractionally larger and then sand the top of the leg at a slight angle so that it goes into the frame with ease and tightens up as it is pushed fully home. I also put candle wax on the leg to make it easier to slide into place.

HINGED TO THE WALL

If the layout is purely a simple track layout with either no scenery or removable tunnels, stations and so on, you simply need to attach a suitable 44mm (1¾in) by 34mm (1½in) batten to the wall and then fix hinges between the batten and the baseboard. This batten must be 100 per cent level for its full length and it must

also be very securely fixed to the wall. This is more of a problem when the property is constructed in stud and plasterboard, than it is with solid walls. If you attach the hinge to the back of the baseboard, the thickness of the baseboard must be less than the thickness of the batten; otherwise it will not fold up flat. If you attach the hinge to the back of the baseboard and create a slight gap between the baseboard and the batten before attaching the hinge to the side of the batten, the baseboard will slope in towards the wall and will be more stable. If you have scenery that is permanently attached, you need to make the batten wide enough to allow scenery to remain in place without being crushed against the wall. As well as making the batten wider, by creating a frame rather than a single batten, you need to provide stops on the wall to prevent the scenery being crushed against the wall. You need to use sufficient 67mm (2¾in) x 102mm (4in) grade 7 washered or ball-bearing hinges to provide adequate support. To fix the board to the batten, stand it upright on the batten with a thin packing in between and then

WEST WILTS MODEL RAILWAY CIRCLE

Solid table top hinged to batten on the wall.

screw the hinges in position to the outside of the batten and the base of the baseboard. If you are not using a solid wood baseboard, the baseboard frame will need some form of strengthening by using 34mm (1½in) softwood rather than the normal 18mm (¾in) for that side of the frame.

You need to decide on an appropriate height before fitting the battens and you also need to ensure that the top of the baseboard does not catch on the ceiling and that it does not catch other obstructions when being folded up. The final stage of construction is to have a catch to hold it in the upright position. The simplest way is to have a piece of wood screwed to a block on the wall just above where the baseboard reaches when folded. This wood is held up when the

baseboard needs to be undone or when it is to be closed. The piece of wood will simply hang down and hold the frame in place. This was the method used in our clubroom for the first few weeks but it has now been replaced with a more complicated system. With very large boards it is possible to fit a rope system with counterweights. If the board folds down rather than up, the track is then exposed and can be easily snagged. The board also has to be sufficiently high off the ground, where it is attached to the wall, to allow it to fold down without hitting the floor. If it folds down, there is also a problem with stowing the legs; whereas if the board folds up, they naturally fold flat against the underside of the board. Instead of legs it would be possible to have a frame with a covering that acted as legs when lowered, but contained a notice-board or picture when folded up against the wall.

Hinged unit folded against the wall. Note how the legs automatically fold flat and the shelf with the controllers always stays horizontal.

Ball-bearing hinge (stronger and easier to operate than a cheaper hinge).

Replacement fastening device – a hook-and-eye rather than the crude length of wood when the board was first installed.

The legs need to be at exactly the same height so that the baseboard is totally level when lowered. The use of a spirit-level is essential. For repairs or alterations to electrics, replacement of point motors and so on, the board can be quickly locked up in a vertical position. Instead of legs, some people place cupboards or shelves in place of the front legs. Whilst this provides extra storage, it does limit access to the board. Even with the board folded into its upright position, you have to lean over the units to work on the underside of the board.

PERMANENTLY FASTENED TO THE WALL

Basically, you need to attach a level batten to the wall, as described above. It needs to be at the height you want the top of the baseboard to be. The simple way is to screw flush mount brackets both to the rear of the baseboard and the front of the batten to create a lift-off mounting system. The legs at the front can be more permanent, as this type of fixing is most useful for fairly permanent fixtures. The two ways to work on the underside of the layout are either to remove the legs and unhook the back from the wall batten or crawl underneath and work upside down (not the easiest of tasks).

Both of the above fixings (hinged to the wall or fastened to the wall) mean that when the layout is in its operational position, there is only access to the layout from the front and possibly the sides.

TRESTLES

If the unit is to be free-standing, there are a variety of trestles available in different guises. There are commercially available sawing horses, which are usually sold in pairs. They have the advantage that they fold flat, but they are only at table height and not adjustable. Telescopic saw horses are available, but they are heavy and extremely expensive. Folding workbenches made by Black and Decker or B&Q are also possible alternatives, as it is possible to make a 'T'-section board and clamp this in the jaws of the bench to raise the height. Apart from the basic saw horse, the others are metal, heavy and cumbersome. They are also more expensive than the option of

IKEA trestle.

wooden legs. Trestles, as well as being available from DIY stores, are also available in a variety of shapes, sizes and prices at a variety of stores, including IKEA. Some of the IKEA ranges have height-adjustable central boards. It is, however, quite simple to make your own trestles. It is basically two matching rectangular frames joined together with hinges at the top.

HINGED LEGS

Legs made out of wood are the cheapest option. They are best made as a pair, as the cross-bars create rigidity. Wood sized 44mm (1¾in) by 44mm (1¾in) is not too heavy, but you can still achieve rigidity with 18mm (¾in) by 28mm (1¼in) legs if it is essential. Rather than using an actual hinge, it is cheaper, yet quite efficient, to just put a bolt through both the leg and the side of the frame. It is important that you either chamfer the top of the legs or ensure that it will not catch during the folding process. Hinged legs can either be permanently attached to the baseboard, which increases weight, or attached and detached

'Hafele' hinge, which lock in both up and down positions.

each time the baseboard is relocated. Hinged legs must be held apart by either opening beyond the vertical or, more effectively, stabilizing the whole unit by having a cross-support from the lower half of the leg to the top of the baseboard. Folding legs have a tendency to drop down when transporting baseboards, unless they are clipped into the closed position, but if you use 'Hafele' folding leg brackets, they produce a hinge that is both strong and locks both in the open and closed positions.

SLOTTED LEGS

The alternative to hinged legs is to create frames on the baseboard corners into which the legs slot, in exactly the same way as described for table-top mounting. Stepped in from the short, stubby legs, I have screwed and glued a further pair of legs. These legs are 900mm (35½in) long to match my other boards and are glued and double screwed. The new legs are made more rigid at the lower end with a cross-member. Because I saved spare wood from previous cuts, I have used the same 18mm (¾in) x 69mm (2¾in). This width is sufficiently wide enough to provide a secure fixing with two screws. Again the joints are glued. It is purely a personal choice, but I

always chamfer the end of the cross-beam, so that it does not catch on trousers, etc., if you are passing close to it. It is not necessary to fix the leg to the baseboard but I usually slide a bolt into a pre-drilled hole through the baseboard side and the leg, just to stop the leg falling out when the baseboard is lifted. There is no need to use a nut to hold the bolt in place. Again these need to be braced between pairs of legs to ensure a rigid structure.

The initial stubby leg described previously in this chapter.

Mark out the width of the bottom part of the leg.

Drill and countersink for two screws.

Clamp the leg at 90 degrees to the plate, glue and screw.

Ensure legs are square to each other and the plate and measure.

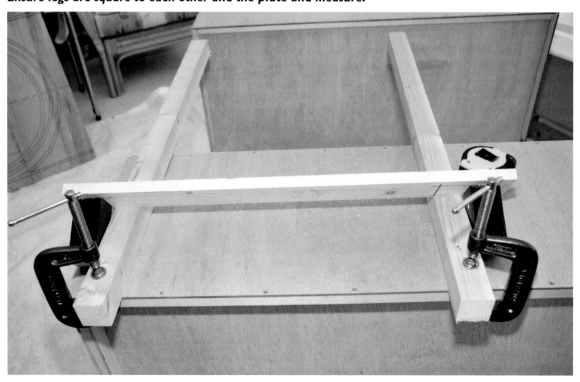

Double check your measurements by marking the lower cross piece near the top joining plate rather than at the bottom of the leg. This will ensure the legs are parallel.

Cut the cross-member to the correct size. I normally mitre the end so that clothes do not catch on a corner.

Glue and screw into place.

Completed leg – but still needs the stubby part of its legs to be chamfered.

Full view of a pair of legs.

SCREW-IN LEGS

It is possible to purchase 870mm (34¼in) high breakfast bar legs or worktop support legs. These have a flat plate screwed to the baseboard. You have to install a strengthening wooden plate to screw the leg plate to it, but then legs can be attached by just unscrewing the central thread on the leg. On some versions it is possible to make small height adjustments, but most are a fixed height. These legs have the disadvantage, as well as cost, that they cannot be attached to cross-supports and rigidity relies totally on the tightness of the leg and its metal plate. They are, however, fairly rigid when tightened.

STABILITY AND CROSS-SUPPORT

Most legs, on their own, are insufficient to stabilize a baseboard. There must be a cross-member between the lower third of a leg and the side of the baseboard. As stated earlier, whether hinged legs or slotted legs, it is best to fix the legs into pairs with two horizontal bars. You only need to add the stabilizing cross-supports to one leg at the front and the opposite leg at the back to ensure stability of a whole length of multiple baseboards.

Screw in legs and plate.

Cross-support made of 6mm (¼in) ply between one leg and the baseboard to stabilize the two boards.

HEIGHT ADJUSTMENTS

Where the home environment is almost certain to have a level floor (although this is not always the case) putting up a layout in a clubroom or at an exhibition invariably involves slight variation in floor levels. Our club room, in an old tannery workshop, has about a 1:30 slope from one side to the other. The best solution is to buy height adjusters for each leg. These metal adjusters simply screw to each leg and can then be raised using a screwdriver to create a level baseboard. There is nothing worse than uncoupling a set of wagons for them to just run away and crash into buffers at the end of the line!

COVERING THE FRONT

To complete the appearance of the layout, most exhibitors add a cloth around the front of the layout, stretching from the top of the baseboard frame to just above the floor. If it goes all the way to the floor,

Height adjuster.

Curtain held in position with Velcro.

it will soon pick up all the dust and need washing. The easiest way to fix this is with Velcro tape. Attach the hooked side of the Velcro to the baseboard side and the other side to the cloth. As you roll it up, the hooks do not hook onto each other as they would if it were the other way round.

CHAPTER TWELVE

LIGHTING THE BASEBOARD

In a normal household situation the baseboard will probably have sufficient lighting from the main room light, although problems can occur when you are viewing the layout. If the room has a single central source of light, your body is more than likely to be between the light and the baseboard, creating a shadow on the area you are viewing. In exhibitions there is considerable uncertainty as to the quality of light and its direction. Exhibition halls are usually filled to capacity with every corner being utilized. The lighting in a whole variety of halls can vary tremendously. Lighting in a church hall and in a gym or dining area will be totally different, as will lighting in a foyer and a corridor. If you are planning to exhibit and wish to display your layout to the greatest effect, the best answer is to provide your own lighting.

If you have your own permanent railway room it is logical to light the room to meet the needs of both the layout and your activities in the room, but if you are operating the layout in a variety of locations, you need to take your own lighting system with you to gain the best effect for your layout.

DESIGNING A LIGHTING BOARD

A well-lit layout attracts people to view your layout and they stay longer. There are a wide variety of lighting systems but your lighting needs to comply with basic rules. Light needs to be above the layout and needs to give relatively even illumination, but must not shine in the viewer's eyes. At exhibitions, if you operate the layout from the back, you need to make sure that the lighting board does not obstruct your eye-to-eye contact with the viewers of your layout. Time after time lighting boards hide the operators' faces from the viewers. In some cases you feel that

this is intentional, as operators in quite a few cases are more interested in operating the layout than in making any contact with the paying public. I understand that, in some cases, exhibitions are the only time that operators get the opportunity to work their full layout, but the most successful layouts have operators at the side or at the front, so that discussions can be opened up with interested visitors.

Posts to hold the lighting gantry need to fix to either the sides of the baseboard or the rear of the board. The gantry needs to be level with the front of the display at a suitable height – usually 800mm (32in) above the track bed. Exhibitors mainly used spot lights, either built in or clipped to the gantry, but with the advent of down lighters and, more recently, with LED lights, lighting gantries are usually slightly smaller than in the past. Each metre of baseboard needs a couple of lights to provide adequate lighting. One way is to construct a box unit the same length as each baseboard, but having one side much longer to provide a shade for the lights and a front for the unit. If installing down lighters in such a box, all the wiring can be inside the box. The top of the box should be ventilated and allow wires to pass along the full length of the gantry box before passing along and down the support to the power supply. All lighting circuits should be terminated with an ELCB (Earth Leak Circuit Breaker) if you are using mains voltage. The inside of the box needs to be painted matt white to give an even spread of light.

The simplest lighting can be achieved with a frame and clip-on spotlights attached, but this tends to detract from the layout and also light can easily shine in the public's eyes.

For my folding layout I have designed a simple lighting gantry, which can be integrated into the folding baseboard unit. When the unit is closed for transportation, the sides with the dowels are joined together with two wooden straps.

The other side of the closed unit is completely flat and the two halves of the baseboard have been joined together with the front and top of the lighting gantry.

THE SUPPORT FRAMES

The first task is to make two support frames out of softwood. The frames are the uprights and they need to be bolted to the ends of the baseboard with coach bolts and wing nuts. One of the frames will need to have a second small frame inserted to support the top of the light stand, which will be slightly smaller than the front (in order to fit inside the stand front when being transported). The supporting uprights are constructed in 18mm (¾in) x

One of the end frames.

Both end frames fitted to the sides of the main board.

The additional frame to accommodate the slightly narrower top of the lighting panel (so that it will sit inside the frame of the front panel).

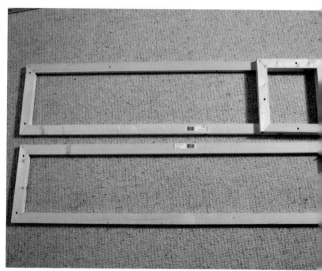

The two slightly different frames.

The two end frames with side panels fitted.

34mm (1½in) softwood. They need to be the height from the base of the baseboard to the top of the front board, plus the viewing height. This will vary according to the height that the baseboard is from the ground, but with a baseboard 1,000mm (39in) from the ground and a front board of 300mm (12in) deep, the frame will need to be approximately 1,050mm (41¼in) from top to bottom. I have made the uprights 260mm (10¼in) wide, So that I do not impair the fixing of any legs and so that the top fits inside the front for carrying.

Identical-sized panels are added to each end to create the ends of the light box. They are the same height as the front panel, which is 305mm (12in) deep and runs the full width of the baseboard. The depth measurement is exactly the same as the width between the outsides of the frames of the two baseboards when they are joined together.

THE TOP AND FRONT PANELS

For the front panel of the light box, the softwood frame is cut to the exact size of the plywood (this can be either a butt joint or a mitre joint). The frame is glued together and then the plywood top is added to the glue-covered frame. Both the frame and the plywood are flexible, and to ensure good contact along the whole length when gluing, I have placed two support beams between the trestles. Unlike a solid worktop it is possible to adjust the width between the beams and clamp the plywood, the frame and the support beam together to ensure perfect contact until the glue dries. When dry, the clamps and the support beams are removed.

CLOCKWISE FROM TOP LEFT:

The front panel frame, glued and resting on beams to permit clamping until dry.

The frame temporarily clamped to the support beams.

The outer frame and plywood front with the top panel frame fitting inside, ready for its plywood cover.

A similar frame is constructed that fits inside the above frame; it is also covered with 3.6mm ($^1/_{16}$in) plywood and will form the top of the lighting gantry. The frame will eventually sit on top of both the front board and the two side upright supports. The plywood top will overhang the frame by 34mm (1½in) at each end and on at least one side. This top is constructed in the same way, again using the support beams until completely dry.

Clamp the front into position, level with the top of the uprights, and drill two holes at each end to allow the front and the frame to be bolted together. The top can be dropped into place and the unit is then ready for painting and the installation of your choice of lighting.

The front panel clamped in place.

ABOVE: *The top panel in place.*

LEFT: *The completed front panel.*

*View from inside
the lighting box.*

*The completed unit
showing the top and
front panels.*

When it is all completely dry, check once again that it will make up and pack away easily. Fit the handles. It may be necessary to re-drill some of the bolt holes as they will probably have acquired a little paint during the finishing processes.

Painted light box.

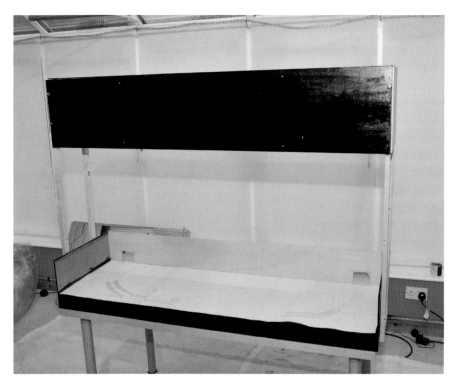

The completed unit.

One of the handles.

The closed unit with the lighting box making up one side.

CHAPTER THIRTEEN

BACKGROUND BOARDS

No layout would be complete without a background scene – the background separates the layout from reality. There is nothing worse than a layout without any background, where the view is of the operator's shirt (or worse). The background should not be so high as to completely obscure the operator, as he needs to be able to see what is happening on the tracks. The background needs to be there but it must either be an integral part of the overall layout or the image should fade into the background and set the scene without it being obtrusive. I do not propose to go into detail about actual background displays, purely to cover the various methods of producing the supports for backgrounds.

There are several ways of supporting backgrounds and I usually prefer to have a removable background to reduce the space needed for both storage and for transport, rather than having a background permanently fixed to the baseboard. The design of the backboard and its fixing will vary according to the layout. As an 'N'-gauge modeller, my backgrounds tend to be 225mm (9½in) high and thus the background board is 300mm (12in) high, allowing 75mm (3in) to be below baseboard level. I normally make my background board from 3.6mm (1/16in) plywood. To give it strength and rigidity I frame it in 18mm (¾in) x 34mm 1½in) softwood. I

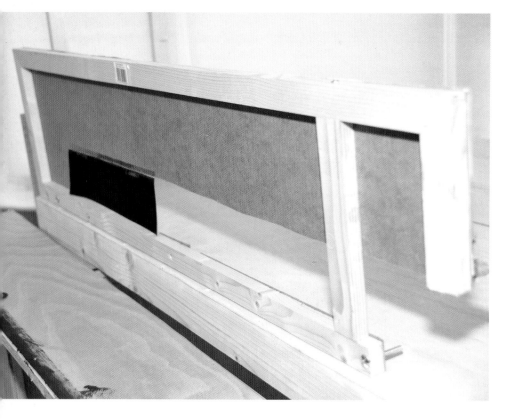

Background board on a frame. Note the cut-out below the road level to allow access and note the black card flap to darken the tunnel entrance.

The tunnel with the flap lifted.

am then able to bolt through the softwood and the backboard to fix it to the baseboard.

On one of my layouts, 'Pendleton Pit', I have a hidden double track in front of the backboard, under a road. This means that the visible backboard is raised to road level. It is likely at some stage that I will need access to the tracks and I

have, therefore, cut away the hidden part of the background board to provide access. This can cause a problem, as the resulting slit allows light down as far as my tunnel entrance. By attaching a sheet of black art paper I have created a flap that allows full access, yet provides the darkness required at the tunnel entrance.

The effect with the flap in its closed position.

The view of part of the background, from the viewing side, with the track going under the road. The houses are fixed to the background scene.

The background removed. The join between the background and the fixed scenery is at the joint of the pavement.

If you have a straight 90-degree join, it can easily be seen. As my row of houses needs some protection, I have stuck the houses and the pavement to the backboard. This means, as can be seen, that the background joint is actually the edge of the pavement. As I am using more than one baseboard, I have made the backboard frame join at a slightly different point than the edges of the two baseboards. If there is a problem with the join of the two baseboards, I do not have two backdrop supports blocking my view.

If you have a rural scene, you can either use buildings or the landscape to hide the join. In my folding baseboard, I have incorporated the background between the two halves of the baseboard; this is fully described in the Chapter 8.

I normally have a background that stretches along the back from end to end and leave the sides open, but some operators prefer to curve the corners, to create more of a diorama. I leave mine straight, as I insert different baseboards to create different scenes and an end baseboard can sometimes end up in the middle. To curve corners you need to use specially cut MDF sheets or thick card, but this really means that the background and the sides need to be permanently fixed and is more appropriate for dioramas.

The off-set frame. This ensures that the baseboard join at track level does not have any background supports in the way – in case of problems.

CHAPTER FOURTEEN

BUYING COMMERCIALLY MADE AND SECOND-HAND BASEBOARDS

BUYING COMMERCIALLY MADE BASEBOARDS

If you feel that you are not up to making your own baseboards from start to finish, there are a variety of commercial options. Obviously, there are companies who will make your baseboard from scratch to finish, and will even design and install a fully wired layout, just ready for you to 'plug and play', but there are others who will do some of the more difficult work for you and leave you to complete the rest yourself. There are some obstacles in doing this and I have devoted this chapter to dealing with these problems and to producing a finished baseboard.

Commercial organizations geared to making baseboards have fully equipped workshops and have standard pattern jigs for use for different sizes. This all makes construction more accurate and more reliable, but quality comes at a price. A birch board

approximately 600mm (24in) by 1,200mm (48in) will be around the eighty pound mark.

The most time-consuming and more complicated part of constructing a baseboard is undoubtedly its sub-frame. It is possible to purchase high-quality frames, cross-members and spines as a kit and then put it together yourself and purchase your own baseboard top. This has the advantage, over doing it yourself, that all the sub-frame is cut to exacting standards with cross-halving joints so accurate that they have to be knocked together with a mallet. With a commercial frame, you make up the spine and cross-members prior to making up the outer frame. The spine and the cross-members are glued before being locked into position. When fixing cross-members and the spine it is essential that they are laid on a hard, level, flat surface before putting any pressure on the strips of wood, otherwise they could either

Commercial workshop. Note the patterns on the wall (the curves are for helix construction).
MODEL RAILWAY SOLUTIONS, POOLE, DORSET

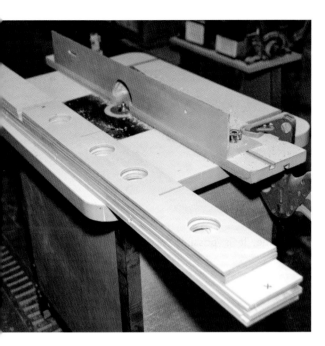

A cut baseboard frame and cross-members about to be packed and posted to a customer.

Cross-members showing the routed slits, where the boards cross over and the holes, which both reduce weight and provide a facility for the wires to pass along the underside of the baseboard.

Pushing the cross-members and spine together. The fit is so snug that a tap with a mallet (only at tap!) is required to ensure the tops are level. To avoid breaking any of the cross-members or the spine, this must be done on a hard, flat surface.

Slotting the cross-members together.

The cross-members with two parts of the frame attached.

The slit in the frame ready for the cross-member to be glued into place. Note the holes for pin nails.

Cross-member patterns on the wall and on the workbench alongside the router.

split or be out of true. It is then a matter of making up the four butt-jointed plywood strips to make up the outer frame. These are glued and pinned through pre-drilled holes, and then the spine and cross-members fit into pre-cut slots in the frame panels. Again, it is purely a matter of gluing and pinning into pre-drilled holes.

You can either purchase the baseboard top from the same supplier or you can have a top cut from standard plywood sheets by your local DIY shop, as described earlier. Fastening the top and the frame to each other needs care. You need to glue the edge of the frame and then line one of the long sides up with the frame and make sure that each end is level. Once you have it correctly lined up, pin each corner and also pin the centre (making sure it is flush with the edge). The next stage is to adjust the frame to line up with the other corners and the other long edge. If you have had the top cut correctly, it will be purely a matter of easing the cross-members, frame and spine into a perfect rectangle. There is always 'give' in such a frame until it is fixed to the top. Do not fix it just as it stands if it is not 100 per cent aligned. If you trim the top to match the unadjusted frame, your board will not be rectangular and the resulting finished boards will not join up correctly, as one board will be slightly skew. It is best to complete the whole process in one go, from making up the frame and cross-members to fitting the top. As with the homemade version, it will need sanding down and varnishing. Sanding will be minimal, as commercial kits or completed boards come ready sanded and some manufacturers say that the wood is sufficiently resilient to damp that sealing it is not necessary.

The biggest problem is that the spine and cross-members fit in pre-determined positions and unless you pay for specialist cutting, you will have to design the position of points, etc., so that they do not clash with the supports underneath the baseboard top, rather than moving the supports to meet the track

design. Some manufacturers will align cross-members to meet your needs, but this is likely to cost extra.

Some companies supply the baseboard in kit form, where you have to put it together, as described above, whilst others make up the baseboard complete with its top and supply it as a readymade unit. Different suppliers use different qualities of wood. The best is multiple-layer birch wood; however, as might be expected, this is by far the most expensive. Cheaper plywood has fewer layers.

The two suppliers I have visited both have a range of different quality materials, which will allow some reduction in price. Some suppliers suggest that one method of fixing cross-members, with partial slots, gives better adhesion contacts than just straight pinning and gluing, as suggested by another. In truth, probably both are so similar that it is actually their cutting system that affects the decision. Routers, for example, are circular and therefore cannot cut a

A lap corner joint in high-quality beech plywood. The lap joint ensures a 90-degree corner and two gluing surfaces. ELITE BASEBOARDS

Another view of a corner prior to gluing, showing bolt/dowel holes at three levels.

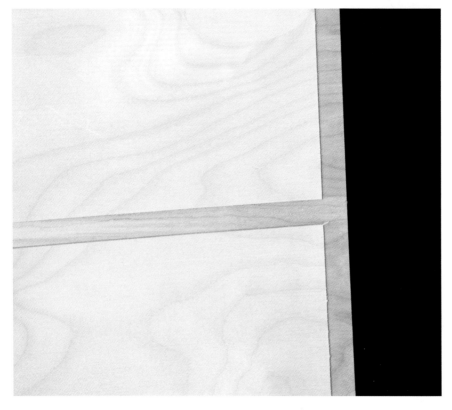

The baseboard top. Note that it is routed out to take the cross-members and provide a good joint between board and frame.

ABOVE: *The side frame routed part way to accommodate the cross-member. Note the shape of the cross-member to match the cut.*

90-degree ended slot, whereas making a complete slot from side to side allows the router to extract a complete slice of the frame. If the glue contact is not 100 per cent, the strength of the frame will be weakened. In fact the actual effect on the strength of a baseboard in normal use is absolutely minimal between either of the systems or purely butt-jointing the cross-members yourself.

If you are on a tight budget, you need to take care when costing out your options. Kits are usually split into frame, baseboard top, legs and cross-supports, and the overall cost of a board can be much higher than at first thought. The production standards are excellent and do represent good value for money and save you a deal of time and effort, as well as giving you an excellent board.

RIGHT: *Full view of routed top.*

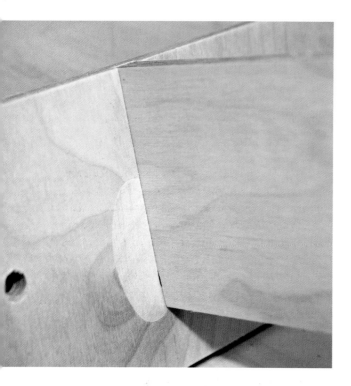

Frame and cross-member glued and joined.

Cut-out holes for dowels at different heights and bolt holes for joining boards.

Both are exactly level and flush at the top.

The finished baseboard – ready to be shipped to a waiting customer.

BUYING SECOND-HAND BASEBOARDS AND LAYOUTS

Buying anything second-hand is always a risk and that risk is totally yours. When I first started in model railways, I purchased a second-hand loco at a show and after a few hours of running it stopped. The cost of replacement of the offending parts was almost as much as the cost of a new loco; since then I have always purchased new locos, but I have purchased many second-hand wagons and coaches, because I can thoroughly check these before purchase.

There are many board-based layouts offered on eBay but you are buying almost blind. You have to remember that someone is disposing of a layout for a reason. It could be a valid reason, but it could be that the layout has many dry joints or that some of the points have intermittent faults, which will cause you no end of headaches, or it could be that an amateur woodworker is working in his garden shed making up cheaply priced passable boards on a part-time basis.

The main points against buying second-hand are that you lose the whole joy of designing and constructing your own layout. You also lose the detailed knowledge of how the wiring has been connected and why it has been set up in a particular way. If you have to replace a point, you have a considerable amount of work to insert a new point or piece of track and to then match the ballast into a seamless join.

The main things to look for are the type and quality of the baseboard top and its frame. You also need to check that it is not warped and that it is level. If the baseboard has a track, you need to check the appearance of the wiring. Is it clearly and cleanly wired or do the wires hang down and look a jumble? If the wiring is fairly tatty or the baseboard looks rough, you are probably buying trouble. If possible, see it in operation before you buy and compare the cost you are paying against the cost of a new layout. It needs to be well over 50 per cent cheaper to make a second-hand purchase worth considering.

Some modellers seem to thrive on buying second-hand equipment, locos, etc., on the internet, finding faults and then buying replacement parts to correct the problem. The result is often that they are paying nearly as much as would have been the cost new, but still they continue to buy in this way.

The advantages are that you have a ready-to-run track and scenery, you don't have to plan a layout, as someone has done the work for you, and you do not pay as much for it as a newly constructed layout. The choice is yours – but beware!

CHAPTER FIFTEEN

BASEBOARDS FOR THE LESS PRACTICAL

The object of this chapter is to show you how, with the aid of a DIY centre with a wood cutting service, you need no more than a screwdriver and glue – you could even get away without the glue!

I would only recommend this style of baseboard if you really feel that you cannot tackle one of the earlier versions in the book. It is a 'quick fix' – something that can be knocked together in a couple of hours with minimal DIY skills.

THE BOARD

The board described in this chapter makes maximum use of readily available materials in standard sizes. It is based on 9mm ($^3/_8$in) plywood and standard lengths of PSE (Plain Square Edged) softwood.

Plywood of 9mm ($^3/_8$in) comes in two sizes: 1,829mm (72in) x 607mm (24½in) and 2,440mm

(96in) x 1,220mm (47¼in). Softwood timber with a depth of 94mm (3¾in) and width of 18mm (¾in) comes in 2,400mm (96in) lengths.

An average board needs to be around 1,200mm (48in) long by 605mm (24in) wide. To achieve this in the most economical fashion, the board measurements referred to in this chapter will produce a board that fits on a frame 605mm (24in) wide by 1200mm (48in) long.

THE CUTTING LIST

- Softwood – 94mm (3¾in) x 18mm (¾in); two lengths 1,200mm (48in) long cut from the length of 2,400mm (96in) softwood with one cut.
- Softwood – 94mm (3¾in) x 18mm (¾in); two sides 571mm (22½in) long cut from a further length of softwood will require two cuts.

The four sides cut to size.

• Plywood – 9mm (³/₈in) is already 607mm (24in) wide and only requires one cut of 1,200mm (47¼in) out of the 2,440mm (96in) by 607mm (24in) sheet – you have enough plywood remaining for a second board or for cutting two 150mm (6in) support squares.

Many DIY centres and wood suppliers offer a free cutting service. The total cost will be (April 2014 prices) under £35.

BUILDING YOUR FRAME

The simple frame uses butt joints. The butt ends of the shorter lengths of wood are joined to the sides of the longer lengths of wood to create an overall width of 607mm (24in).

Before you do anything more, lay the top on the floor and place the four pieces of frame in position as though the baseboard was upside down. Check that when fixed, the whole unit will come together and that neither the measuring nor the cutting is incorrect. When you are happy, your next job is to bore two holes, one above the other, in each end of the lengths and use a countersink.

Glue one end of a side, insert 50mm (2in) screws and tighten.

Repeat the process on all the other corners until you end up with an oblong frame 1,200mm (47¼in) by 607mm (24in). Do not wait for this to dry but continue to the next stage. You will need eight screws 50mm (2in) long.

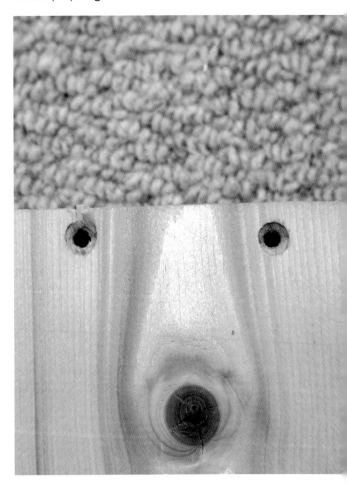

Butt joint.

Two holes and countersink.

Completed frame.

FITTING THE TOP TO THE FRAME

Lay the top in position and again check that it all fits (do not worry if it is not entirely square). Slightly move the board so that it overhangs the frame on two sides and drill a series of pilot holes with a 2mm ($^1/_{20}$in) or similar drill bit, on both the overhanging sides and also use a countersink on each screw. The holes should be about 100mm (4in) apart. Move the top so that it overhangs on the other two sides and repeat the process. This stops the drill entering the frame and will give better grip if the screw is entering new wood, rather than a pre-drilled hole in the frame.

Make sure you have your screwdriver and enough 20mm ($^3/_4$in) screws – you will need about thirty. Starting on one corner, line up the top with the corner, and the one side and one long length. Insert a screw in that corner and loosely tighten. At the other end of the longer length make sure that the top is lined up and insert a screw in that corner. Staying on

Glued end of frame.

Offset baseboard top.

Drilling the board.

Corner screw.

Pushing the frame into square.

the same side, ensure that the frame is in line with the edge of the baseboard in the centre of the frame and insert a third screw. Tighten all three.

Move to the opposite side and push the frame into square with a corner and again repeat the process with the other corner and the centre of the long side before tightening the screws.

When you are happy that everything is lined up, correctly insert and tighten up alternate screws right round the board until they are all in place.

Wipe away any excess glue and put the board face up on a hard, flat surface, with paper underneath to catch the glue. Weight the board down and leave until dry.

Your baseboard is now complete apart from sanding down, painting and inserting legs. For sanding and painting, I suggest you follow the instructions in Chapter 9.

LEGS

You can, of course, follow the instructions in Chapter 11, but the simplest way is to fit screw-in legs. Legs designed for breakfast bars are readily available from DIY warehouses and can be simply screwed to the underside of the 9mm (^{3}/$_8$in) plywood or, to gain extra strength, you can get your spare ply cut into four 150mm (6in) squares. Glue one side and two edges of these squares and place them in each corner. Using 20mm (^{3}/$_4$in) screws, fix the leg plate in the corner. This length of screw will go through the plate and almost through both 9mm (^{3}/$_8$in) layers of plywood. Leave the baseboard upside down until the glue is dry.

Finally, screw the legs in place.

COMMENT

I can only repeat that the board will be a little heavy and a little chunky, but it will be solid and can be achieved with the minimum of tools and expertise.

Placing the glued squares in position.

The plate screwed into position.

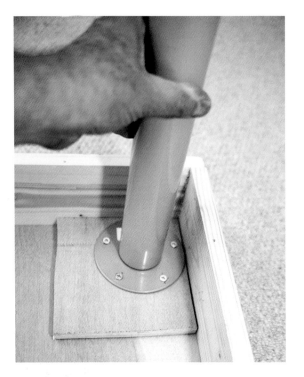

ABOVE: *Screwing in the leg.*

JOINING BOARDS TOGETHER

In previous chapters I have explained how to link boards together using dowels. I have explained how the dowels need to be sunk into the frame using a spade drill. In this chapter, I show a simpler way of getting a flush fit without the use of a spade drill. Fortunately the depth of the base plate of a dowel is almost the same thickness as 3.6mm (¼in) plywood.

If you line up the two baseboard ends and clamp them together, then bore a guide hole as per previous instructions on fitting dowels, you can then screw the dowels directly on to the frame. This will leave them both standing proud of the frame and when joined, there will be a gap. By cutting a narrow strip you can screw and glue a piece of 3.6mm (¼in) plywood above the dowel, level with the top of the baseboard.

BELOW: *The finished baseboards forming the base of the new West Wiltshire Model Railway Circle's 'N'-gauge layout.*

CLOCKWISE FROM TOP LEFT:

Dowel and 3.6mm (¼in) plywood.

Plywood fixed above dowel but level with baseboard top.

Plywood additionally fitted between the dowels to ensure baseboards clamp together level and accurately.

To ensure there is an even fit, you also need to add plywood between the two dowels and at either side, otherwise the two end plates will not sit level.

The two baseboards can be clamped together with either bolts drilled through both frame ends or with toggle clamps. The baseboard tops will now provide a level, joined-up bed for the tracks and the boards will be locked together in just the same way as if you had drilled the end frame with a spade drill.

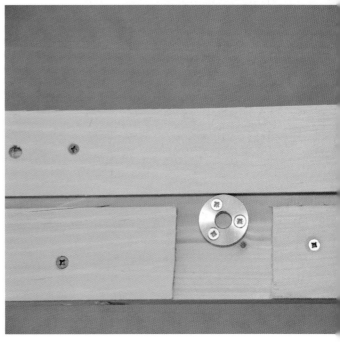

CHAPTER SIXTEEN

CONSTRUCTING A HELIX

The helix is not really a baseboard. It is usually a circular structure that sits on top of a baseboard to raise trains from one level to another. Proportionately, the helix takes up a massive amount of space and is fairly costly and difficult to make. It is also complicated and requires a considerable amount of mathematical calculation before construction can begin.

CALCULATIONS

First, you need to know the height to which you wish to raise the track. In 'N' gauge you need to divide this height by 50. In raising the track in a spiral you need 50mm (2in) clearance between track levels to permit finger access, in addition to the track and the train. In 'OO' it needs to be 100mm (4in). The maximum

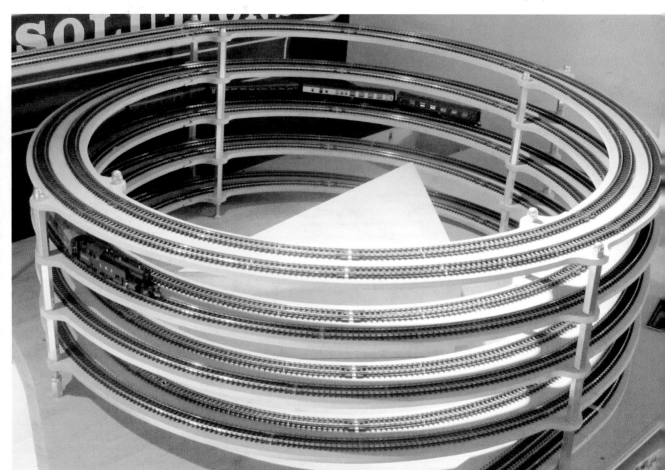

A commercially constructed helix exhibited by Model Railway Solutions.

slope must be less than 1:50; therefore, to achieve each lift of 50mm (2in) in N gauge, the circumference of the middle of the two tracks must be 1,000mm (39in).

To obtain the radius you require for a 50mm (2in) lift, the 1,000mm (39in) is divided by 3.142 (Pi):

(3.142) = 318mm (12½in)

My baseboard is 700mm (27½in) wide, therefore, the maximum radius I can have is 340mm (13½in) to allow a little clearance at the side. Digging back in my mind to my schooldays, the circumference of a circle is 3.142 (Pi) times the radius:

3.142 x 340mm (13½in) = 1,068mm (85in)

This means that for every 50mm (2in) rise I need one complete circle. As I wish to have a rise of 125mm (5in), I need two and a half lifts of 50mm (2in).

Having measured the curved spacing required in planning previous track layouts, I am aware that the width between tracks on a tight curve of 340mm (13½in) radius needs to be 30mm (1¼in). Tracks are 10mm wide each and there needs to be an overhang of 15mm on each side, giving a total minimum width of the track platform of 80mm (3¼in). To give greater clearance I have allowed a 100mm (4in) wide track bed.

The next task is to draw out a full-sized diagram of the circle on wallpaper lining paper and then check that the two tracks fit comfortably, with space for supporting and joining the track bed.

DRAWING AND MARKING OUT

As in previous drawings of curves, use a pencil, a drawing pin with string tied between the two, initially at 350mm (13¾in) (the outer circumference) and second at 250mm (9¾in) to draw the inner circumference.

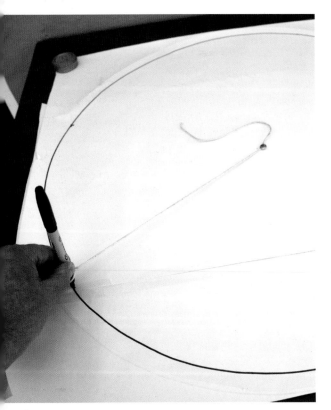

Using string and a felt tipped pen to draw the circle.

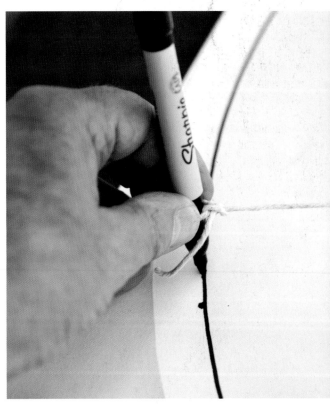

String tied to pen. Winding the string will achieve the narrower circle.

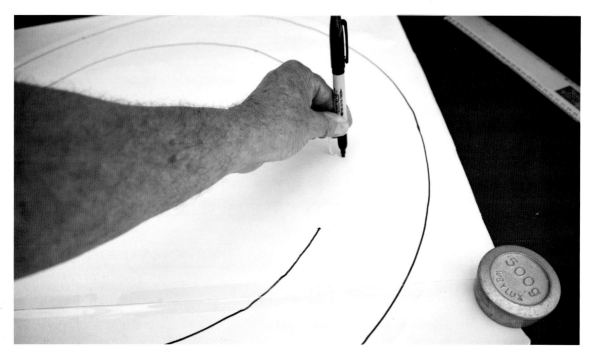

The narrower (inner) circle almost complete.

To save wood, and to make life easier, each circle can be made from two semicircles. To achieve the height, I need three semicircles plus two semicircles with a run on/off straight of about 100mm (4in).

Once drawn on to paper, add notches, as shown, to hold the vertical supports. Cut out the circle, then cut it into two. You then need to transfer the patterns, interlocking as shown, to 6mm (¼in) plywood. Two of the semi circles need 100mm (4in) straight sections added to the template to form the entry and exit from the helix

With 6mm (¼in) plywood being 607mm (24in) wide, the best standard length to purchase is 1,829mm (72in). The cuts required can be achieved from one sheet. However, they cannot be cut commercially as all the semicircles interlock to limit the amount of plywood used. If you are planning a different height of lift, you can lay the cut paper semicircles on a flat surface and, ensuring you keep within the 607mm (24in) width, work out the exact size of plywood required. Plywood also comes in lengths of 2,440mm (96in) and 1,220mm (48in).

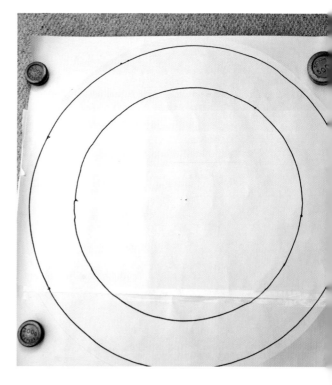

The two complete circles (the paper is weighted down to stop it rolling up).

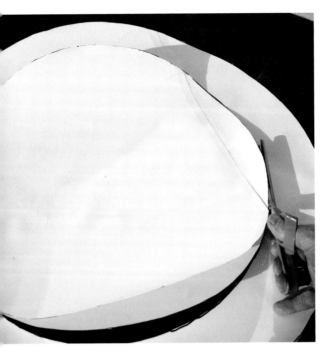

Removing the centre of the circle.

The paper cut-out of the circle.

Cutting in half to create the cutting plan.

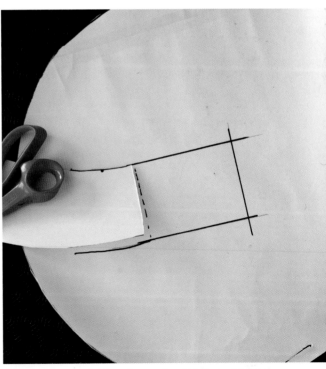

Adding the straight entry and exit pieces to one of the halves to provide the template for the entrance and exits pieces of the helix.

CUTTING AND SANDING THE SEMICIRCLES

I have recently purchased a fret saw and I wrongly assumed that this would be better for cutting the semicircles from the plywood sheet. However, the length of the arm was insufficient to allow the wood to be turned at the right angle to make the required cuts and I soon resorted to a jig saw with a fine blade to cut out the shapes. I used the workbench and gradually turned the wood so that it was in close contact with the edge of the bench throughout the cut.

Having been cut, each edge needed sanding and this is where the detail sander came into its own to reach the corners of the support notches.

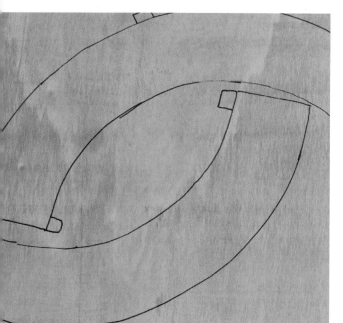

CLOCKWISE FROM TOP LEFT:

The plan drawn out on a sheet of plywood. Note the layout to minimize use of wood.

Two sections of plywood cut-out. Note the addition of notches on both the inside and the outside of the track bed. These notches will be drilled to hold the support threads which hold the helix upright and correctly spaced.

All five cut-outs – two with extensions for entry and exit.

Using a detail sander to cope with the internal curve. This is nor possible with any other type of machine sander.

A detail sander coping with the difficult notch.

Sanded shapes ready for painting. The table is covered with plastic sheet and then newspaper to prevent any paint spilling on to the table itself.

Paint the edges first and then fill in the middle. It is probably best to handhold the plywood whilst doing the edges to ensure good coverage.

PAINTING

The individual semicircles have to be hand-held for most of the painting. I covered the table with a polythene sheet and then newspapers, then laid out the various pieces prior to picking each one in turn and, holding it by hand, painting the edges first and filling in the flat area with it laid on the newspaper. To get an even finish, once all the area is covered, you need to run the brush from end to end rather than leaving it with different levels of paint.

As soon as each one was painted, I placed a small block under each piece to raise it off the newspaper so that it did not stick.

Once there is a coat of paint on one side, run the paintbrush from end to end to get an even spread and even finish.

The five semicircles raised off the paper and left overnight to dry. They are all resting on small blocks of off-cut wood.

When dry each piece was sanded to remove any paint that had spilled to the opposite side and then this second side was painted and left for a day to dry. There were small areas on the edges that had not been fully painted, so each of the semicircles was hung over the workbench and the edges touched up and again left to dry.

When the other side has also been painted and dried, rest the wood on end (I have used a workbench) to touch up any missing parts on the edges.

CONSTRUCTING THE HELIX

The next task is to cut the supporting poles. These are M6-threaded rods, usually available in 1,000mm (39in) lengths. I needed eight to support the helix and they had to lift the track up over 150mm (6in). As I needed two lengths of rod, I opted for a length of 250mm (9¾in), which allowed for fixing under the baseboard and plenty to spare for increasing the height, if required. It would have been possible to cut each rod to the exact length required, but as the difference is only 25mm (1in), I followed the same pattern as commercial builders and cut all the rods to the same length.

The next task is to lay out all the semicircles on the baseboard and then drill through all the nodules and the baseboard in one go. This ensures that the rods will line up correctly.

With all the rods screwed into position you need to line up the nuts that will support the first rising bed. There is a lead in from baseboard level and then

Threaded rods come in 1,000mm (39in) lengths. I needed two lengths cut into 250mm (9¾in) pieces to form the threaded poles to support the track bed. After measuring I found it best to have a nut each side of the cut. This held the saw roughly in place and, when the cut was complete, unscrewing the nut removed any burr.

Lay the cut track beds out on the baseboard in the exact order they are to be fitted.

Drilling the holes in the nodules on the track bed and through the baseboard to take the threaded poles.

a rise of 1:50 throughout the helix. The first nut is a few centimetres along the track bed from baseboard level and needs to be about 5mm (1/8in) from the base. By the time the first circuit has been completed, the track needs to have risen by 50mm (2in), hence the nut on the left of the picture is set to hold the end of the first complete circuit.

Although I knew my measurements were correct, I always prefer to physically check that things will go where they are supposed to go – hence the loco and track. Satisfied that everything fitted as planned, the next task is to insert a joining plate. This is placed over the two rods and the two adjoining semicircles are glued to this plate and clamped until dry. (The illustration shows an unpainted plate, but this is just for photographic clarity.)

Construction continues until the helix is complete. The joints have been left unglued at this stage to show that the track beds are under tension and because of the lift and the twist, they do need to be joined together. The best way is to glue them and then clamp them with a bulldog clip until dry – normal clamps are a little too large!

The baseboard with the threaded poles fixed by washers and nuts.

Setting to the nuts to support the helix track bed. The nut on the left-hand pole is only a few millimetres from the ground-level as this is the first support for the entry track bed. The right-hand pole will support the higher level of the first completed circuit of the helix, hence it is 50mm (2in) higher. The fitted track beds are shown in the next picture supported by these nuts and poles.

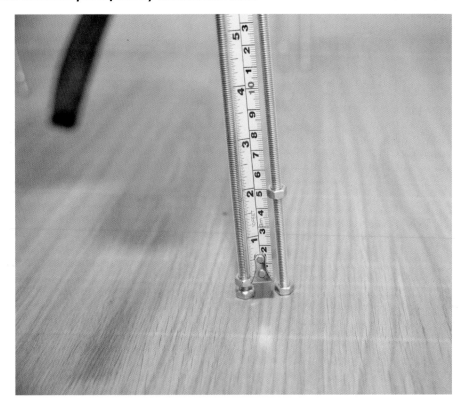

With the first two half-circle boards complete, I placed a small amount of track and a loco at the end of the first circuit to verify my calculations were satisfactory.

A typical joining strip, which fits between the two bolts and under the two boards at each half-turn.

The additional risers are added including the 'off-ramp'. Both the on and off ramps and the gradually rising track bed are clearly visible.

As boards are both twisting and rising, they need to be glued to the joining strips.

They are then clamped until dry.

All that remains now is to slide and glue the two tracks into position on the helix, but that is not part of building a baseboard. One tip is to use strips of this wood, just wider than the width of the track bed, and two bulldog clamps to hold the glued track in place until dry. A further tip if using flexible track, is to stagger the joints of each side of the track, so that each rail keeps the angle of curvature in turn.

USEFUL ADDRESSES

B&R Model Railways
14, Weedon Road, Aylesbury, Buckinghamshire HP19 9PE
– baseboard manufacturers

The Gas Cupboard
6, St George's Works, Silver St, Trowbridge, Wilts BA14 8AA
01225 777888; www.gascupboard.co.uk

Elite Baseboards
80, Forest View Rd, Tuffley, Gloucestershire GL4 0BY
01452 720599; www.elitebaseboards.co.uk

Model Railway Solutions
Unit 1 10 – 12 Alder Hills, Poole, Dorset BH12 4AL
01202 798068

Model Scenery Supplies
15, North Norfolk Business Centre, Northrepps, Norfolk NR 27 9RQ
 – baseboard manufacturers

Parkside Electronics
Unit 3E and 3J Valley Mills, Southfield St, Nelson Lancs BB9 0LD
 – baseboard manufacturers

PECO
Underleys, Beer Devon EX12 3NA
 – track plans and track, etc.

Professional Layout Services
831 Mansfield Rd, Nottingham NG5 3GF
 – baseboard manufacturers

Ron Pybus
25, Bratton Rd, West Ashton, Trowbridge Wiltshire BA14 6AZ
01225 774440; pybus@btinternet.com

Station Rd Baseboards
9, Station Rd, North Elmham, Dereham, Norfolk NP20 5HH
 – alignment dowels and baseboards

White Rose Modelworks
Unit 10 The Craft Yard, Bedale Station, Bedale, DL8 1BZ
 – baseboard manufacturers

BRM Guide to building first model RR.

Station Road Baseboard
Cabinet makers Dowels.
(alignment tools)

N gauge

INDEX